THE NEW INVISIBLE HAND

THE NEW INVISIBLE HAND

FIVE REVOLUTIONS IN THE DIGITAL ECONOMY

KYLE T. WESTRA

NEW DEGREE PRESS

COPYRIGHT © 2019 KYLE T. WESTRA

THE NEW INVISIBLE HAND

Five Revolutions in the Digital Economy

ISBN   978-1-64137-264-0   *Paperback*

          978-1-64137-265-7   *Ebook*

To Amanda and Eva

CONTENTS

"...led by an invisible hand to promote an end which was no part of his intention."

—ADAM SMITH, *THE WEALTH OF NATIONS*

INTRODUCTION

My grandfather, Thomas M. Thompson, operated a parking garage and several Avis Rental Car locations in and around New Haven, Connecticut for most of his professional life. His father, my great-grandfather, had had a repair shop servicing cars in the area, aside from during World War II when the shop was converted to machining ammunition shell casings for the war effort.

Automotive, in other words, was in my grandfather's blood. He enjoyed knowing the industry and took particular pride over his polished blue Cadillac convertible. He took even more pride in his grandchildren; to let us climb all over that car, he must have.

In early 2011, my brother and I were visiting and had a new company to tell him about: Zipcar. Founded a decade earlier, Zipcar enabled short-term and last-minute car rentals with its fleet of vehicles.

Unlike a traditional rental company, Zipcar focuses on rentals by the hour or even minute. Rather than keeping a centralized lot, Zipcar has its vehicles dispersed throughout a city. Zipcar charges for membership, and additionally members pay only for time used. Gone are the days of needing to book a car for an entire day just for a short trip.

Zipcar co-founder Robin Chase, responsible for multiple transportation-based start-ups, sees the industry as fundamental.

"Transportation is the center of the world!" she exclaimed. "It is the glue of our daily lives. When it goes well, we don't see it. When it goes wrong, it negatively colors our day, makes us feel angry and impotent, curtails our possibilities... What's not to love?"[1]

We knew my grandfather, though long retired, would agree with Chase. I was looking forward to him getting a kick out of Zipcar's innovative model.

As my brother and I explained the concept, a bemused smile crept onto our grandfather's face.

"Never," he said, shaking his head, tickled.

Running a rental franchise was stressful and took long hours. The idea that a decentralized and location-less service like Zipcar could ever work seemed impossible to the seasoned automotive man.

I nearly jumped in to reply, but he continued, listing all manner of issues with Zipcar's business model.

"How could there be enough demand to keep the cars in use?"

---

1   Schawbel 2012

"How could downtime be managed when providing short rides?"

"How could they keep the cars clean and running?"

"What about insurance? Who is responsible?"

"I'm sorry, but I just don't see how this idea could ever work," he concluded. "It's fanciful."

These were legitimate questions, and I didn't know the answers to them. But, as we didn't have the heart to tell my grandfather, Zipcar was *already* working just fine in many cities.

Later that year, Zipcar would have its initial public offering (IPO) and enjoy a market capitalization of over $1 billion.[2] Two years later, it was purchased by the Avis Budget Group, quite a coincidence for my grandfather. Today in 2019, Zipcar operates in over 500 cities and 600 college campuses across 10 countries, serving over one million members.[3]

With Zipcar, technology had enabled something that was truly a paradigm shift from what was possible before. And in turn, Zipcar today is facing stiff competition from ride-hailing companies such as Uber and Lyft, a concept as unimaginable to proponents of Zipcar as Zipcar itself was to traditional rental services.

---

2   Primack 2011

3   "Zipcar Overview | Zipcar Press Center" 2019

We are in the beginning stages of a powerful economic revolution, the likes of which the world hasn't seen for hundreds of years.

THE STATE THEN

Economist and philosopher Adam Smith published *The Wealth of Nations* in 1776, a time of great change in his native Scotland and throughout the world. Mechanization and industrialization were upending traditional agricultural societal structures.

The world was changing faster than at any previous point in history, going back to when the Agricultural Revolution ten thousand years before brought about the advent of civilization itself. Smith saw that in his time, just as before, individuals, organizations, nations, and markets would have to adjust.

Historians describe the period in Great Britain from 1760 to 1840 as the Industrial Revolution.[4] Smith therefore was writing from the vantage point of only the beginning of the transformation.

Whereas no one with any certainty could have said where this revolution would end, Smith correctly identified the major changes happening in economics, business, and market organization. Consequently, *The Wealth of*

---

4   "Industrial Revolution" 2019

Nations has been regarded as the foundation of modern economic theory.

In it, Smith introduces the concept of the "invisible hand." He uses this metaphor to refer to the unseen forces that organize economies, motivate commerce, and determine how goods are allocated. Markets and outcomes appear directed, as if by an invisible hand, but are in fact the unplanned outcome of millions of uncoordinated decisions.

My grandfather gave me his 1937 copy of *The Wealth of Nations* around the time I moved to Chicago, where I would work for a few digital companies, get my MBA, and finally begin working in pricing strategy. It stayed on my bookcase, prominent but unopened for several years, always next on the list of books to read.

He passed away in 2015 at the enviable age of 96, at home and surrounded by family. Some time after the funeral, I flipped through his book, curious if he had made any margin notes or other personalizations to its contents.

The pages were unmarked, but there was one interesting finding. A single slip of paper, stamped with his name, marked the page on which the invisible hand quote appears.

"...led by an invisible hand to promote an end which was no part of his intention."[5]

---

5   Smith 1937

Evidently, this line stuck out to my grandfather as well. It got me thinking more about the changes he witnessed in his life and the ones I was already starting to notice in mine.

THE STATE NOW

We are at the beginning of another great transitional period in business. While the Industrial Revolution was driven by mechanization, the Digital Revolution is driven by information. Digitization and communication technology, especially the internet, have turned the world upside down.

While the Digital Revolution has brought with it countless benefits, the dangers to existing businesses and manners of conducting commerce are readily apparent.

- The median CEO tenure at large-cap companies was five years as of 2017, reflecting a steady drop over the years.[6]
- Many industries are becoming more concentrated, with fewer companies claiming a larger percentage of market share than ever before.[7]
- More than 50% of small businesses fail in their first four years, illustrating the difficulty of finding a stable business model.[8]

---

6   Marcec 2018
7   OECD Secretariat 2018
8   Sweetwood 2018

- At the same time, the lifespan of large companies is shrinking. Whereas the average tenure of a company in the S&P 500 was 33 years in 1965, it was only 20 years by 1990. By 2026, it is estimated that this lifespan will dwindle to only 14 years.[9]
- And the average age of S&P 500 companies has dwindled from 60 years in the 1950s to less than 20 years today.[10]

The pace of change in the business environment is faster than ever, thanks in large part to the Digital Revolution. With so much dynamism, the costs of corporate missteps are higher than ever too.

"Big companies in any moment always look like behemoths that you will never be able to compete with," says Sam Altman, entrepreneur, investor, and president of the wildly successful startup accelerator Y Combinator. "And 10 years later, it always looks so obvious about how they got beaten."[11]

We are often unable to see the potential behind innovation until it's too late. Even people intimately familiar with a certain industry, such as my grandfather, are no exception.

---

9   Mochari 2016
10 Sheetz 2017
11 "Sam Altman On Loving Community, Hating Coworking, And The Hunt For Talent (Ep. 61—Live)" 2019

WHY THIS BOOK

James R. Schlesinger, economist and senior public official, opined, speaking as the U.S. government: "We have only two modes — complacency and panic."[12]

As Director of the CIA, Secretary of Defense, and our first Secretary of Energy, Schlesinger was only too familiar with the tendency of large organizations to become inured to "business as usual." When times are good, there is no reason to change. When times are bad, there's no *time* to change.

My goal with this book is to shake you out of complacency and, perhaps, to assuage your panic.

I started my career at the Center for Strategic and International Studies (CSIS), a nonpartisan foreign policy think tank in Washington, D.C. I researched global trends and helped to convene leaders from government, business, the military, and nonprofits to discuss the challenges they all faced. Getting various perspectives in the same room to analyze economic and security issues was invigorating, but lacked the immediacy of working in business.

When I transitioned away from foreign policy, I thought my trend analysis days were behind me. But as a strategy consultant, I again get to meet with leaders to help them think through their most pressing issues and execute improvements. Thanks to the vantage point I have

---

12 "Quotation of the Day" 2005

with Wiglaf Pricing, I've witnessed new trends over the past several years that led me to the ideas behind this book.

The challenge for executives and organizations, in global affairs as in business, is to recognize obstacles and opportunities in advance. Additionally, the value behind synthesizing the findings of disparate experts and experiences of various organizations turns out to be very real in the corporate world as well.

The idea that the business landscape is changing at an unprecedented speed is not new. Executives and commentators have noticed it for years, but we've lacked a common understanding of how the different pieces fit together and how to prioritize new information.

This book presents an overarching framework to explain just that and to demonstrate how to position your company for success. Too many organizations seesaw between complacency and panic, never realizing that the opportunity to improve is always there for the taking.

THE NEW INVISIBLE HAND

The forces of innovation that are affecting the way goods and services are bought and sold represent one of the greatest threats — and opportunities — to all businesses today.

Over the past two years, I've spoken to dozens of business founders, leaders, researchers, experts, and entrepreneurs to uncover the innovations shaping the future of how we price everything. Their insights and experiences are critical to understanding that the effects these revolutions are having are only just beginning.

While not only forcing me to reframe the way I see the world, it became clear that there are five major revolutions poised to reshape pricing and business strategy as a whole:

- **Reintermediation**: How the role of much-maligned middlemen is changing, with new online intermediaries upending entire industries and finding new ways to bring value to customers. We'll see how many leading companies are seizing such opportunities.

- **Monetization**: New applications of pricing models to hone in on your target customers and the importance of pricing discipline. How the price of a single cup of coffee hamstrung a café in Washington, D.C. and lost the business tens of thousands of dollars a year in profit.

- **Transparency**: Promise and peril for your business. How changing expectations force companies to be proactive in how they communicate with customers. How one company found that more transparency wasn't always better for its customers.

- **Channel**: Deciding who can help you reach your customers (and who is merely in the way). We'll meet, among others, a dealership-less car company and a food startup that didn't want to be available in the grocery store.

- **Data**: The new oil of the Digital Revolution. Data requires careful strategy and refinement to unlock its full value.

Learn how certain companies are doing it well, and how others are falling behind.

These forces combined constitute nothing short of a revolution in how companies must create value for customers and stay ahead of the competition. Understanding these forces and how different companies are adapting is critical to maintaining and increasing profitability.

Smith's invisible hand referred to the unobservable forces that guide the actions of customers, suppliers, and entire marketplaces. Supply, demand, and price allocate scarce resources and organize industries.

Reintermediation, monetization, channel, transparency, and data represent the New Invisible Hand. They are an additional layer to Smith's concept. Unleashed by the Digital Revolution, these hidden forces increasingly determine who gets what, when, how... and at what price.

At Wiglaf Pricing, I have the pleasure of working with many leading companies in their industries. I've seen how these forces are affecting not only single firms but their entire commercial ecosystems. They are challenging.

But good companies can survive despite them. And great companies can thrive *because* of them.

WHAT YOU'LL LEARN

Throughout this book I will share principles, strategies, techniques, tools, and use cases that make it easier to compete in this changing business environment. My goal is not only to describe the current state of affairs but also to provide actionable concepts for capitalizing on opportunities.

With the right framework for thinking about these revolutions, executives will be better equipped to evaluate new industry information and technological developments strategically, rather than get caught up reacting tactically to the latest craze. Structure reduces ambiguity and assists in decision-making under uncertainty.

In this book we'll uncover critical developments such as:

- How intermediaries are flourishing by finding new ways to create value, and what that means for your industry
- How to identify new opportunities for monetization and applications of different variable, dynamic, and personalized pricing models
- How transparency in price and pricing are upending marketplace dynamics but can represent both promise and peril for your company
- How eschewing the channel relationship status quo can open up new and exciting methods for demonstrating brand value and increasing customer engagement
- How data has become the lifeblood of companies that want to make informed decisions about their customer relationships and pricing

- How these five revolutions point to simple principles for thriving in the digital economy

We will meet companies and executives who are already taking advantage of these new developments, as well as ones that are failing to create value and falling behind the competition.

The New Invisible Hand may be intangible, but it isn't unknowable.

Part I

REINTERMEDIATION

Chapter 1:

THE BIRTH OF DIGITAL REINTERMEDIATION

"[O]ur pace of digitizing life has been increasing at an exponential pace."

—CRAIG VENTER, BUSINESSMAN AND
BIOTECHNOLOGIST JOINTLY RESPONSIBLE FOR
FIRST SEQUENCING THE HUMAN GENOME[1]

THE WRONG STORY

In 1995, Bill Gates was on top of the business world. Microsoft was only three years away from becoming the largest company on the planet. The launch of its Windows 95 operating system was a veritable global phenomenon. Customers queued up to purchase it, much like they might today for the latest iPhone.[2]

That year, Fortune wrote that Gates and fellow Microsoft founder Paul Allen "had the will and drive to create

---

1   Venter 2008
2   Titcomb 2015

more wealth than any business partners in the history of American capitalism," calling them "the undisputed masters of the digital universe."[3]

Also in 1995, Gates published his book *The Road Ahead.* Futuristically sold with a companion CD-ROM, the book summarized his thoughts on the personal computer revolution and predictions for the still nascent information superhighway that today we simply call "the internet."

In his book, he predicted that the internet would "extend the electronic marketplace and make it the ultimate go-between, the universal middleman... in which market information will be plentiful and transaction costs low."[4] Gates saw a bleak future for middlemen, or *intermediaries,* in the digital economy because the internet would make such connectors obsolete.

Even wildly successful business leaders and visionaries make bad predictions, however. And Gates got the future of intermediaries completely wrong.

* * *

For many years, thought leaders and technology pundits predicted that the internet would lead to the death of intermediaries. This process is called *disintermediation.*

---

3 Gates et al. 1995
4 "Imagining The Internet" 2019

In this story, business intermediaries primarily help customers find producers and sift through large amounts of information. Since the internet greatly reduced the cost of information and connecting, customers would no longer need help making purchase decisions. With all the world's information at one's fingertips, everyone would know what to buy.

Gates isn't the only luminary to have imagined this bleak future for intermediaries.

Esther Dyson, a prominent angel investor and businesswoman, claimed in 1997 that "[i]t's going to be very difficult to make money as a middleman on the Internet."[5]

Award-winning political and business journalist James Fallows argued in 2004 that the internet's "long-term impact on middlemen is clear": the internet will make them irrelevant.[6]

And Om Malik, the founder of technology media company Gigaom, wrote in 2014: "Whether it is through stock-market trading or the sale of hotel rooms, the internet has a way of bringing deflationary forces to all businesses that were hitherto inefficient and involved many middlemen."[7]

There are multiple problems with this story, however. As we'll see, the Digital Revolution hasn't caused wide

---

5   Lohr 1997
6   Fallows 2004
7   Malik 2014

disintermediation. If anything, the role of intermediaries has only increased.

This churn and tumult amongst middlemen is called *reintermediation*.

THE GROWING IMPORTANCE OF INTERMEDIARIES

"Middleman" often has a negative connotation because of the impression that such entities aren't performing a true service, only taking a slice of the pie and making the overall product or service more expensive. "Cutting out the middleman" is a common mantra of entrepreneurs looking to improve a market.

Conventional wisdom on the value of intermediaries suffers from at least three flaws:

- First, it betrays a very narrow view of the services that intermediaries provide. We'll explore all of the different roles in which we can find middlemen adding value.
- Second, it misses the fact that despite a wealth of information in the Digital Age, humans still have limited time and energy to review it. Customers today need more help making purchase decisions, not less. We live under the so-called "tyranny of choice," with so many options it can be overwhelming.
- Third, as data increases, so does misinformation, making the separation of the signal from the noise harder than ever. Knowing who and what to trust is a full-time job.

Whereas intermediaries accounted for 25% of U.S. GDP in 1999, by 2010 they already accounted for 34%. The incredible growth of internet-enabled intermediaries is a large reason for this.[8]

Many of the world's most powerful and dynamic companies are digital intermediaries. The *Harvard Business Review* reported in 2017:

> *Five of the 10 most valuable companies in the world today— Apple, Alphabet, Amazon, Facebook, and Microsoft—derive much of their worth from their multisided platforms (MSPs), which facilitate interactions or transactions between parties. Many MSPs are more valuable than companies in the same industries that provide only products or services: For instance, Airbnb is now worth more than Marriott, the world's largest hotel chain.[9]*

And these MSPs are nothing but a form of intermediary, as we will see shortly.

Whereas traditional intermediaries have suffered, new ones have come to take their place. Those traditional ones that have survived have had to adjust to a radically different business environment.

Once we understand the different roles intermediaries fulfill, it becomes easier to see how different types of

---

8   Krakovsky 2015a
9   Hagiu and Altman 2017

intermediaries add much more value to the market than it may appear.

* * *

"My ears always perk up when people say they're going to cut out the middleman. In many cases, cutting out the middleman simply doesn't happen," Marina Krakovsky said to me.

Krakovsky is a social science and business journalist and author of the 2015 book *The Middleman Economy: How Brokers, Agents, Dealers, and Everyday Matchmakers Create Value and Profit.*[10] In this book, she examines the changing role of middlemen in the digital economy and provides a useful framework with which to identify the types of value a middleman company is providing in different situations.

Her six categories of middlemen are:

- **The Bridge**: These are the types of middlemen most commonly thought of, those that connect two groups that otherwise may not find each other. An example of a Bridge is eBay, which unites buyers and sellers in disparate locations, or the MSPs that the *Harvard Business Review* referred to.

- **The Certifier**: Certifiers help bring trust to the marketplace via information. They, through their expertise, can

---

10   Krakovsky 2015b. Many of the ideas in this chapter are explored more in depth in this excellent book.

help guide others through the consideration and buying process. Think of Yelp, whose user ratings can make or break a restaurant.

- **The Enforcer**: Enforcers bring the muscle. They help maintain compliance for all parties. Wedding planners have an Enforcer aspect: their presence incentivizes suppliers to do a good job even if a particular flower supplier won't see a particular bride and groom again.

- **The Risk-Bearer**: Risk-Bearers do just that: manage risk and uncertainty, specifically exogenous risk. Whereas self-publishing a book may sound great in theory, there is a lot of uncertainty involved regarding marketing. Publishers, among other tasks, accept the costly risk that the book may fail (most do)[11] and in turn earn a considerable amount of the profits if the book succeeds.

- **The Concierge**: A Concierge has domain-specific knowledge and experience to help organize and execute matters better than a layperson. Travel agents fall into this category, and while the internet has dramatically changed this industry, there is still a lot of value in saving people the time and hassle of self-organization.

- **The Insulator**: Insulators, instead of bringing people together, keep them apart. While this seems counterintuitive, think of lawyers and agents who allow strategic

---

11   Ballentine 2014

interactions between two parties that would be harder to achieve directly.

Many companies assume more than one of these roles. And many companies aren't truly aware of all the roles that they fulfill for their customers. It isn't necessarily better for a company to cover more roles than fewer, but each role represents a customer need and therefore an opportunity to provide a service.

Understanding Krakovsky's six types of middlemen illustrates how language that is dismissive of intermediaries ignores the real and growing importance of such services in the digital economy. As we've seen, many of the best known digital companies today are intermediaries, at least in part. And profits abound for companies that are able to seize the opportunity of reintermediation.

In this section, we will take a closer look at various cases of reintermediation. We will see the peril it represents for traditional businesses and the promise it holds for those able to capitalize on it.

Predictions about the death of middlemen got it exactly backwards.

KEY TAKEAWAYS

- Contrary to conventional wisdom and past predictions, intermediaries are not disappearing. In fact, they are only becoming more important to customers and the economy as a whole.

- Krakovsky's framework is a useful way to think about the various roles that intermediaries can play between a supplier and a consumer.

- The common perception of intermediaries as simple Bridges overlooks the multiple ways in which they add value to markets.

KEY QUESTIONS

- If your company is an intermediary, what role(s) does it fulfill?

- Is your company's intermediary role misclassified by certain customers, or perceived as only one type of intermediary when in fact it serves multiple valuable roles?

- Are there unfilled roles in your industry that could be ripe for action?

Chapter 2

INNOVATING ON TRADITIONAL INTERMEDIARIES

"There are technologies that open up opportunities that would otherwise be impossible, inefficient, or cumbersome."

—*SCOTT CASE, FOUNDING CTO OF PRICELINE*

The Digital Revolution has enabled a new generation of companies to improve upon the services that traditional intermediaries offer.

In this chapter, we will see how multiple digital intermediaries have upended industries by taking advantage of new technological possibilities.

STEALING NEWSPAPERS' CROWN JEWELS

In 1997, two years after Bill Gates's *The Road Ahead*, a two-decade veteran of the media conglomerate Tribune Company named Mitch Golub could feel a change in the air. He was attending the Newspaper Association of America's annual convention in Chicago. Giving a particularly tumultuous speech was none other than Gates himself. But what was Gates doing at a newspaper convention?

"There was a huge audience, over a thousand people in the room," Golub recalled for me. "And Gates, whose voice squeaked quite a bit when he got animated, basically said to the publishers: Come up here and kiss my ring, or I'm going to steal your crown jewels."

Those jewels he referred to were the papers' classified advertising sections. For decades, newspapers had been a major source of advertising for the automotive industry, real estate, and job hiring. As a whole, the U.S. newspaper industry made $41.3 billion from advertising in 1997, and classifieds were a major part of that.[1]

Gates directly threatened this lucrative business model. Microsoft was ascendant, and its owner saw the potential in online services. Newspapers' classified advertising would move online, and traditional publishers could either get on board or be left behind.

His pronouncement "launched a shouting match," Golub said. The audacity of a computer nerd, even a very successful one, challenging newspaper industry experts on their home turf caused a frenzy.

"When all the yelling and screaming died out," Golub said, however, "three of the companies there decided to do something about it."

---

1   "Estimated Advertising And Circulation Revenue Of The Newspaper Industry" 2018

The Tribune Company, the Times Mirror Company, and the Washington Post Company recognized that Gates was right: he could decimate print classified advertising. It didn't matter if they were upset by Gates's words; it was up to them to adjust to a new business reality.

As Professor Michael C. Munger of Duke University argues: "Economic revolutions don't care what we think about them."[2]

These three companies decided to work together on a product that would enable them to defend their classified advertising. They and other traditional industry players weren't without advantages, of course. After all, they had substantial resources too. Brand recognition and reputation are hard-won and take time to create. They also had much more familiarity with the classifieds industry and local market dynamics. Such incumbents who recognized the shifting business landscape should have a considerable leg up on Microsoft, a software company starting in advertising from square one.

The joint product of the *Tribune*, *Times Mirror*, and *Washington Post* companies became Classified Ventures, the media group responsible for sites such as Apartments.com and Cars.com. Golub became the first employee and president of Cars.com in July 1997.

---

2   "Michael Munger On Sharing, Transaction Costs, And Tomorrow 3.0" 2018

I would meet Golub at Cars.com eighteen years later as an MBA intern and then employee. By some stroke of luck, my cubicle was mere feet from his president's desk. I literally had a front-row seat to his work.

The thinking was, Golub said, "We will have the advantage. We can build a national brand for traffic, but sell and promote to local customers." And that is still largely what Cars.com does.

The site provides automotive manufacturers and dealers with the online presence they need to reach local customers via branding and advertising. Customers can browse local inventory, communicate with dealerships, and make more informed purchase decisions. Cars.com became a strong national brand to draw in interested customers, thus increasing its value with manufacturers and dealers and creating a positive feedback loop.

Cars.com serves a purpose similar to newspaper advertising, but does it much better. For prospective car buyers, it provides an easy way to cut and compare inventory at a very detailed level across any number of dealerships, as well as compare prices, check reviews, and communicate with dealers. For dealers, Cars.com provides an audience much more targeted than the average newspaper reader, who more likely than not isn't even in the market for a new vehicle. It also provides targeted insights and digital tools unlike anything a newspaper could offer.

Recalling Krakovsky's framework from the last chapter, Cars.com is fulfilling more than just Bridge functions (connecting buyers and sellers) as a newspaper classified section might. It is also providing Certifier (supplying ratings and reviews) and Concierge benefits (providing research and pricing guidance) as well.

Over the course of nearly twenty years until his retirement, Golub steered the company into over half a billion dollars in annual revenue based on a simple insight. Technology had opened up a new and better way of both providing advertising services and helping shoppers find a vehicle.

In this case, Gates was right. The internet *would* eat traditional newspaper advertising.

The fate of the newspaper industry since then confirms this. From a high of $49.4 billion in 2005, the U.S. newspaper industry's annual advertising revenue crumbled to $16.5 billion in 2017, an amount not seen in nominal dollars for over 35 years.[3] Revenue levels that took 50 years to grow crashed in just 12 years.[4]

Cars.com and companies like it largely took classified advertising away. Behemoths such as Google and Facebook have dominated other types of online advertising. Advertising wasn't disintermediated, but *reintermediated.* This example is illustrative of how the Digital Revolution

3   "Trends And Facts On Newspapers | State Of The News Media" 2018
4   Ingram 2013

has enabled technology companies to fulfill a similar role that traditional intermediaries did but do so in a much better way, providing more value to both consumers and producers.

About half of Cars.com's growth came after 2004, when the site began entering newspaper markets not owned by the media parent companies, Golub told me. These newspapers that had adopted a digital strategy were able to gain a substantial edge over their peers.

"We were in every major local market within two years, and we rarely met with any real resistance from the newspapers," Golub said. "Reintermediation spawned a strategy that allowed Cars.com to generate hundreds of millions in revenue and profitability from markets in which they never initially intended to be."

MAKING COUPONS COOL

Before my stint at Cars.com, I found myself in Chicago with no clue as to what kind of job I would find. I moved from Washington, D.C. to Chicago in 2011, following my future wife and looking for a new path after my few years in foreign policy studies. I applied to dozens of jobs at various corporations, nonprofits, startups, and universities, but heard nothing back.

It turns out that, understandably, no one outside of D.C. knew what a "think tank" was, let alone what to do with someone whose only work experience was at such a mysterious organization.

The only nibble I received was from Groupon. This was fortunate for many reasons. First, and crucially, someone wanted to hire me! Second, I was excited about the company. I had been fascinated by its explosive growth and used it frequently as a customer. Third, I knew I was going to learn a lot very quickly.

Groupon serves as a great example of the new type of intermediary being created by the internet. Customers wanted to explore businesses and activities in their community, but information was scattered, biased, and difficult to collect. Businesses needed to find a way to pierce through the preponderance of information online and appeal to the right customers.

Cars.com was one example of moving newspaper advertising online, but Groupon was an entirely new beast. Whereas newspaper ads or billboards had served similar needs in the past, Groupon promised to promote and organize local commerce by creating buzz around local businesses with flash sales, as well as create new demand through special promotions.

These sales depended on an intermediary such as Groupon collecting what were in effect promises from shoppers. The merchant agreed to offer a deal if and only if a certain critical number of customers agreed to put money down. Recalling this chapter's opening quote from Priceline's

Scott Case, such a system would have been very cumbersome if not impossible to create before widespread adoption of the internet.

"Most small business owners are not particularly sophisticated business people," Groupon's founder and CEO, Andrew Mason, said in 2012. "That's not a criticism; they're passionate about cutting hair or cooking food, and that's why they got in the business, not because they have an MBA."[5]

The world was changing, and the only way to survive was to digitize. "We've succeeded in making coupons cool," said Mason.[6] With that, Groupon spawned a daily deals industry that, despite waning in popularity from its exuberant highs, has reached revenues of $6 billion in 2019 in the U.S. alone, reflecting steady year over year growth.[7]

SIMPLIFYING CAB HAILING

It was also in Chicago that I first experienced the beginning of our current transformation in urban transportation options.

Walking my dog near Washington Square Park one morning, I saw a car go by with a giant fuzzy pink

---

5   "Groupon Head Andrew Mason: 'We've Succeeded In Making Coupons Cool'" 2012

6   Ibid.

7   "Daily Deals Sites Industry In The US" 2019

mustache affixed to its front grill. It was 2013, and Lyft had arrived in the Windy City.

I first experienced app-based ride hailing with Uber in Boston that spring after a downtown music festival. A friend arranged a black car via his iPhone, and we were whisked to his home in Cambridge while most people were still furtively trying to hail a cab. It truly felt futuristic.

Lyft, at the time, was slightly different in that its drivers all used their personal vehicles. (For those who don't remember, Uber started out by only using premium black cars before throwing its weight behind UberX, its own version of what Lyft provided.) Lyft felt more personal that way, and the big fuzzy pink mustaches on the front of many of its cars made the service feel low-key and fun.

Logan Green, co-founder of Lyft, put a lot of emphasis on expanding to Chicago. "It's a big launch for us," he said at the time.[8] As a San Francisco-based company, Lyft entering Chicagoland was a big step away from home and toward having a national presence.

Lyft and Uber are examples of new intermediaries made possible only by the Digital Revolution. For such ride-hailing services to work, there are many technological pieces that need to fit together. Accurate street mapping, GPS, and smartphones are all necessary. Without any of those, ride-hailing couldn't function.

---

8   Rodriguez 2013

Fast forward to 2019, and Lyft has cemented itself across the U.S. Its March 2019 IPO revealed 2018 revenue of $2.2 billion, double that of 2017. It has nearly 20 million active riders across 600 U.S. cities with an eye toward international expansion.[9]

These markets are served by over one million drivers. I met one of those drivers in Denver recently, picking me up from the airport after a work trip.

"I work 20, 25 hours a week. Any more than that and it starts to feel like a job!" My Lyft driver smiled widely.

The driver, who I will call Angelo, has been driving for Lyft and Uber for the past couple of years, tallying up nearly 5,500 rides by his own account. Retired from the hospitality industry, Angelo supplements his and his wife's savings by driving with Lyft and Uber. He won't be old enough for several more years to qualify for Medicare, so he has health insurance to pay for. He makes enough driving to cover that and have some spending money left over.

"Thank you in advance for the Caribbean cruise my wife and I are taking this summer," he said, chuckling.

I was sitting in the front passenger seat for our ride and noticed a cane in the footwell. "Henry," Angelo called it, "is one of my close companions." Not only does it help Angelo get around, but he also was wielded the cane on

---

9   Carson 2019

one occasion to protect himself from a drunk and belligerent passenger.

"This guy tried to pull me out of my own car," Angelo said. "And he did it, he got me out, but not before I grabbed Henry."

"I clapped this guy once on the side and then solidly on the head. He left me alone after that. Man, my heart was racing."

At first glance, the intermediary function of Lyft and Uber is simple. They fulfill what Krakovsky calls Bridge roles, connecting riders to drivers. These are also called "two-sided platforms." Through the Lyft and Uber apps, people who need a ride and people who offer a ride find each other.

When Angelo and Henry fought off the belligerent passenger, the encounter left Angelo unharmed but spooked. The assailant was a young man, and Angelo is not. The incident easily could have gone in a different direction.

Had Angelo been driving a cab, this could have been the end of the story. The assailant stumbled off into the night, so neither Angelo nor the cab company would have had a way of identifying the man.

But Angelo and his passenger had been connected together by Lyft as an intermediary. Both needed an account on the service to do so. Lyft knew *exactly* who was in Angelo's car at that moment.

Lyft therefore became an Enforcer in this transaction as well. It could penalize the man for his behavior or even bar him completely from the service. Lyft has a strong incentive to ensure that *all* of its drivers are protected from passengers' bad behavior, not just the one driver who is directly affected.

Lyft solicits a rating for each ride from both the driver and the rider on a one to five star scale. If the driver rates the rider as a three or below, the driver will never be matched with that particular rider again.[10] At the very least, Angelo will not to have to deal with the same man in his car again.

On the rider side, Lyft has stringent expectations for its drivers as well. "If your rating is below 4.8, you may want to consider ways to improve it. Consistently low ratings can put you at risk of deactivation," Lyft tells its drivers.[11] Imagine if a product on Amazon were at risk of being removed for less than a 4.8 rating!

As well as being an Enforcer, Lyft is also a Certifier, creating trust between two strangers so that both sides of the market don't need to think twice about using the service. The incredible growth in ride hailing demonstrates how primed the market was for this technological development.

---

10   "Driver And Passenger Ratings" 2019
11   Ibid.

DISRUPTING TRAVEL AGENCIES

It would be natural to think that the founder of two wildly successful startups in the same industry might have a particular interest in the sector. But for Priceline's Scott Case, his focus is almost accidental.

"For me, the industry is less interesting than the scope and scale of the potential opportunity," Case told me.

Case became the founding CTO of Priceline, the innovative discount travel booking site, in response to such an opportunity. I asked him if there was something in particular about travel that excited him in the beginning.

"No," Case paused. "Actually, it still doesn't, as crazy as that sounds. But the scope and scale of making travel booking easier turned out to be enormous."

This wasn't the answer I expected from someone responsible for the technology behind one of the first truly disruptive digital travel intermediaries. But for Case, travel just happened to be the right field at the right time.

"The fundamental approach is more about discovering a set of insights, understanding what's possible, and evaluating where those insights are best applied," he explained. Priceline was the application of these strategies.

If a hotel room goes unfilled for a given night, that inventory has expired; the hotel cannot sell that room for that night ever again. The same goes for an empty airline seat or unsold concert ticket. The practice of pricing such expiring inventory is known as revenue management. (We will return to revenue management in Chapter 8: Dynamic Pricing.) As long as the hotel can cover the variable costs of servicing that room, filling it is profitable for the hotel, even if at a steep discount.

There are a few dangers, though, in such steep discounting. A hotel may have a certain brand image that would be hurt by too many price concessions. Customers may become unwilling to pay full price if they regularly see discounts available. Discounts given at the last minute may encourage all customers to delay their purchase as long as they can. And determining which customers are happy to pay full price and not providing them with a discount is very tricky.

Priceline solved these problems for hotels with a new technological invention called the "conditional purchase offer." This innovation enabled the company to handle previously impossible transactions between customers and suppliers. Such an offer is, in effect, a binding agreement between a buyer and seller on price, so long as certain conditions or criteria are met. For a hotel, that may be a certain mile radius from a given area (for the buyer) and an offer above a certain minimum price (for the seller).

Priceline enabled customers searching for accommodations to set a price at which they would be happy to have a hotel room, and hotels could then match that price if interested. Crucially, when a customer agreed to a transaction on Priceline, the specifics of the hotel wouldn't be visible. This protected hotels' brand image and hid the price concession from regular customers. Hotels could fill rooms at a discount with targeted, time-sensitive, individual offers. This solved hotels' massive revenue problem of having empty rooms expire and enabled customers to get deals on accommodations.

This breakthrough offer mechanism was marketed as *Name Your Own Price®*. Priceline capitalized on its technological advantage and clear value-add to both sides of the transaction in order to enjoy enormous growth. Comparison shopping was prohibitively difficult before the emergence of online two-sided platforms that could aggregate and present data in a useable format from all kinds of providers.

In terms of intermediary roles, Priceline's value comes not only from Bridge activities but crucial Risk-Bearer and Enforcer presences as well. The company uses its substantial market presence to encourage good behavior on both sides of the transaction.

The work of Priceline beforehand would have been accomplished by the individual buyer or by travel agents. The number of travel agents in the U.S. declined from 124,000 in 2000 to 74,000 in 2014.[12] The U.S. Bureau of Labor Statistics expects a further decline of 10,000 travel agents between 2016 and 2026.[13]

---

12 Lam 2016
13 "Travel Agents: Occupational Outlook Handbook" 2019

Only two years after its founding, Priceline went public at a valuation of $11.8 billion. Now known as Booking Holdings, the parent company also includes such properties as Booking.com, Kayak.com, and OpenTable.[14] All together, Booking Holdings earned $12.7 billion in revenue in 2017.[15]

Picking up the phone to call a travel agent would never occur to the vast majority of travel customers today.

DIGITAL REINTERMEDIATION

Cars.com, Groupon, Uber, Lyft, and Priceline are all examples of digital intermediaries that capitalized on new possibilities heralded by technology and digitization. These intermediaries are also examples of two-sided platforms because in order to succeed they must add value to both sides of the equation: producer and consumer. Both producers and consumers are customers of the intermediary.

These companies serve as intermediaries between a producer and a consumer, disrupting existing intermediaries with new and better services:

- Cars.com provides advertising and promotion to car manufacturers and dealerships on the one hand while offering prospective car buyers a better way to shop, reintermediating newspaper classified advertising.

---

14   Weber and Petersen 1999
15   Sorrells 2018

- Groupon serves both businesses looking to promote themselves and consumers looking for a deal, disrupting local print and broadcast advertising.
- Uber and Lyft (in their most popular manifestation) are platforms for drivers to find riders who need transportation, and vice versa. This has significantly supplanted existing taxi services and affected all other forms of local transportation, such as buses and subway systems.
- Priceline enables travel and hospitality providers to fill discounted inventory strategically while giving budget travelers a way to save. Travel agents are one traditional intermediary group that has lost out due to these developments.

Cars.com and Groupon replaced existing Bridge intermediaries with expanded services. Ride-hailing technology created a new market by serving multiple intermediary roles. Travel agents already provided Bridge and Concierge activities, but Priceline could do more, at scale, and with specialized pricing tools.

Such companies do not make a product in the traditional or obvious sense. But they also do much more than simply connect consumers and producers to each other. It is critical to understand all their sources of value to appreciate their importance. All of them are pioneers in their industries for introducing new digital ways for consumers and producers to interact.

As we will see in the next chapter, none of these industries have stood still. Such digital intermediaries are facing their own disruption in turn.

KEY TAKEAWAYS
- Traditional intermediaries are being replaced with digital intermediaries that solve the same or similar customer problems, in a better and cheaper way.
- The process of intermediaries disrupting other intermediaries is called reintermediation.
- Continued digitization of intermediary functions is very disruptive, but also provides many opportunities for companies that can seize them.

KEY QUESTIONS
- Which traditional intermediaries in your industry are being disrupted or have already been replaced?
- If your company is a traditional intermediary, how are you adapting to digitization and/or mitigating the damage caused by new entrants?
- What opportunities are there in your industry for a digital intermediary?

Chapter 3

REINTERMEDIATION OF DIGITAL INTERMEDIARIES

"Disruption is a process, not an event, and innovations can only be disruptive relative to something else."

—CLAYTON CHRISTENSEN, HARVARD BUSINESS
SCHOOL PROFESSOR AND PIONEERING
MANAGEMENT CONSULTANT[1]

The previous chapter focused on cases in which digital intermediaries have been disrupting traditional intermediaries by creating more value for their customers.

The Digital Revolution is far enough along, however, for multiple generations of digital intermediaries to appear. Newer entrants are often reitermediating *already digital* competitors.

---

1   Denning 2015

BUYER (AND SELLER) BEWARE

The first generation digital marketplace is typified by Craigslist, an online platform for buying and selling all manner of goods and services. Its interface is clean and simple, with its text-heavy design barely changed since going live in 1996. It largely serves as a Bridge in Marina Krakovsky's categorization, connecting people who want to conduct commerce but otherwise staying out of the way.

It works well, but mostly operates under buyer-beware (and seller-beware) guidelines. If a transaction goes south, Craigslist has little to no role in mediating.

While this is sufficient for a number of customers, we have seen an explosion in the number of sites and services taking a piece of the online marketplace pie. They do this by having a different focus from Craigslist and serving different customer needs.

"Companies like Airbnb have really set the bar high, and standards are rising," Krakovsky explained. As it turns out, most customers want more than bare-bones service.

Before Lyft and Uber, Craigslist was a popular tool for organizing rideshares within cities. Such postings are still present, but a huge volume of users clearly prefers the added level of service of such ride-hailing apps. We know this because when the city of Austin banned such services in 2016, tens of thousands of riders and drivers moved to coordinating on Craigslist and Facebook as the next best thing.[2]

Customers like to know that they can trust a marketplace. Ensuring compliance in a transaction is something that a very hands-off service cannot provide. This is a downside of pure Bridge intermediaries. And if there are downsides to a service provider, that means that there are opportunities for other entities to provide a different level of service.

Ride-hailing services are also disrupting intermediaries such as Cars.com by means of disrupting car ownership itself. Owning a car is neither the status symbol it used to be nor a requirement for modern urban life. The number of teenagers obtaining a driver's license in the U.S. and U.K. is falling steadily.[3]

Let's look at just a few more of the hundreds of cases in which digital intermediaries themselves are reintermediated by new services.

HARMONIZING MUSICAL INSTRUMENT SALES

What do trading stocks and selling musical instruments have in common? Quite a lot, according to David Kalt, founder and CEO of Reverb.com, an online marketplace for musical instruments. And he should know, having

---

2   Davidson 2016
3   Naughton and Welch 2019

previously been the CEO and co-founder of optionsXpress, an online trading platform sold for $1 billion in 2011.[4]

"Good stocks retain value over time or go up. So do most musical instruments. This isn't buying and selling doohickeys that lose all their value," says Kalt.[5]

His moment of realization that led to Reverb occurred while he was trying to run a retail music store in Chicago. Despite his love of guitars and all things music, the limitations of a brick and mortar store became apparent to Kalt.

Knowing the advantages of a digital platform, Kalt looked online. While customers could buy and sell instruments on sites such as eBay and Craigslist, it wasn't a good process. General e-commerce sites made it difficult to find and categorize inventory according to how a musician would think.

"I realized I had to build a better marketplace than eBay for musical instruments," remembers Kalt.[6] He was also done with the retail store model of selling his own inventory. In 2012, Reverb.com launched as a dedicated marketplace for users to buy and sell musical instruments and accessories. And marketplaces are intermediaries by nature.

"I thought it would be a $50 million or $100 million business—fun," he says.[7] This level of fun is already matched,

---

4   Jamieson 2011
5   Foster 2017
6   Ibid.
7   Ibid.

with Reverb bringing in around $60 million in revenue in 2018 on $600 million in transactions.[8]

How can Reverb command such growth and sales when, objectively, any transaction it facilitates could have been accomplished on Craigslist? It does so by fulfilling more intermediary roles.

While Craigslist's bare-bones approach works for some users, it has also opened an opportunity for services like Reverb to offer more. Musical instruments tend to be expensive, hard to ship, and subjective in value. To encourage commerce through its platform, Reverb takes responsibility for mediation. On its website, the policy reads:

> *In the case of a dispute, Reverb will contact the seller directly to help broker a return or refund for the fastest possible resolution. If resolution cannot be reached, we will help the buyer obtain a refund through one of several avenues.*
>
> *If payment was made through PayPal, we will walk you through their claim process and, if needed, provide materials necessary to ensure this process reaches the correct end.*
>
> *If payment was made via Reverb Payments, we will issue a refund directly to the buyer's credit card if we are unable to find a reasonable solution with the seller.*

---

8   Dallke 2018

If you are unhappy with your purchase in any way, please fill out this form and our Resolutions Team will get back to you within 48 hours.[9]

That's a lot of work! But it's very valuable in assuaging the concerns of buyers and sellers who want a little more assistance than what Craigslist offers.

In Krakovsky's parlance, Reverb is assuming much greater Certifier and Enforcer responsibilities. Customers who recognize the value in higher value service will pay for it.

This was the situation I found myself in when I needed to part with my Martin D-16GT dreadnought guitar. I wanted more for it than I could get from a retail store, but I also wanted more service than I would get with a posting on Craigslist.

Being dedicated to musical goods, Reverb also has a more targeted user base than generalist eBay, increasing my odds of a good sale. I had treated the guitar well over ten years, but the guitar had some light wear and tear. Reverb made it easy to share detailed pictures of the guitar, making it clear to potential buyers what they would be getting.

With the site layout emphasizing detailed photos and Reverb's resolution dispute mechanism, I felt more

_____

9   J 2018

confident that any transaction would proceed smoothly. The buyer would know exactly what they were purchasing. Buyers too would have greater confidence that I wasn't misrepresenting the guitar I had for sale.

Reverb takes a cut for their Certifier and Enforcer responsibilities, one that I was happy to pay in order to have a smoother transaction. Its thriving marketplace demonstrates that I am not alone.

DISRUPTING PROFESSIONAL SERVICES

Krakovsky has personal experience with many intermediaries thanks to her writing, editing, and consulting work. One such site is Reedsy, which helps people connect to writers and editors for tasks such as self-publishing.

Traditionally, book publishers take a hefty cut of book proceeds in order to offset the work they do and the risk they take. Writers who self-publish take on those responsibilities themselves.

"Self-publishing is an attempt to cut out the middleman," Krakovsky explained to me. But, as it turns out, self-publishing is hard. The entirety of the process is still daunting. There are a lot of moving pieces to organize for an aspiring author to go all the way from concept to physical book.

The internet has provided all manner of digital tools to help prospective writers develop a manuscript and self-publish. Assistance with every step in the writing, editing, and publishing process can be found on simple online marketplaces such as Craigslist. Whereas self-publishing was supposed to cut out intermediaries, in reality it has spawned new ones instead.

But a simple Bridge isn't ideal for such high-value services. Most customers would like to have more background on the person they're hiring (Certifier). They'd like some assurance that the work will be quality (Enforcer). A new breed of digital intermediaries such as Reedsy have popped up to assist.

If you need an editor, designer, or other professional for your project, Reedsy is there to help. Reedsy displays the full name, overview, and writing credits of its service providers. This makes sense; when someone hires for these services, they want to know who they're getting. (Contrast this with a site like TaskRabbit, which doesn't reveal the full names of its "Taskers" in order to keep buyers and sellers transacting on its site.)

Such services could be acquired via a bare-bones Bridge marketplace such as Craigslist. But especially for high-value and particular work like writing and editing, many customers want increased trust and compliance. Reedsy is there to provide these Certifier and Enforcer roles. It has raised over €1 million from investors who see promise in their model.[10]

---

10 "Reedsy | Crunchbase" 2019

DISRUPTING ONESELF

In 2015, Scott Case found himself at a crossroads. He'd left Priceline 15 years earlier, having helped bring it to $1 billion in sales in under two years. His next startup, however, fumbled and failed.

"It was a humbling experience," according to Case, whose Main Street Genome startup had attempted to create products through which small businesses could leverage their own data streams to improve their businesses. Regarding the period after which he shut the company down, Case says: "Honestly, I was self-diagnosed as clinically depressed for a while."[11]

Licking his wounds, he wound up back in the orbit of Priceline's founder, Jay Walker, and their mutual long-term friend Jon Ellenthal. It occurred to Walker and Case that their work in the travel industry wasn't over yet. This time, their target was set specifically on business travelers.

In 2015, Walker, Ellenthal, and Case started Upside Travel, which helps business travelers save money and hassle. At Upside, the key realization was the fundamental misalignment in the interests of the buyer (the business traveler) and the payer (the traveler's employer or client).

Such a situation is a riff on the classic principal-agent problem from political science and economics, in which there is a separation in duties and incentives between the

---

11   Hodges 2017

entity that makes a decision (the agent) and the entity on whose behalf the agent works (the principal).

"The employee makes all the decisions, and the employer deals with the consequences," Case said.[12] A business traveler who pays for a flight using company money is not incentivized to make the most cost-effective purchases.

After Priceline, Case once again saw "an opportunity to really reimagine how travel is purchased and make the entire process easier for everyone involved."[13]

And if Upside can reduce the gap between the agent and principal, then it is saving the principal real money. It can collect a share of those savings as its fee.

Upside fulfills many intermediary roles. Similar to Priceline, Upside is at least a Bridge and Enforcer. To this, it adds substantial Risk-Bearer services by providing 24/7 customer support for its business travelers who cannot afford travel hiccups. It also serves as a Concierge by taking the hassle of managing itineraries and bundled purchases off of its customers' hands.

Its target users (business travelers at small and medium-sized businesses who travel a half dozen times a year), may have used Priceline previously to Upside; there is at least some overlap between the two companies' customers.[14] But the real disruption the founders of Upside are

---

12   Ibid.
13   Ibid.
14   Korosec 2016

bringing to their own previous digital intermediary is with additional Risk-Bearer and Concierge services.

AMAZON

Perhaps the greatest example of digital reintermediation belongs to Amazon. What started out as an online bookstore has a market capitalization of nearly $1 *trillion* as of March 2019 and regularly vies with the likes of Apple and Microsoft for most valuable company in the world.[15]

Tellingly for the future, Amazon is especially popular with younger shoppers. It can claim a full 97% of millennials as its customers, and nearly two out of three millennial shoppers do at least 50% of their online shopping on the site.[16]

This would be astounding for a company that merely connects buyers and sellers. But, of course, being a Bridge is far from all that Amazon does today. The company that began by simply selling books has become "The Everything Store," as named by journalist Brad Stone in his book of the same name that details the company's rise.[17]

But even the word "store" is misleading. Amazon does so much more than many marketplaces, let alone any simple store. Test yourself: how many of Krakovsky's intermediary categories does Amazon fit into?

---

15 Owens 2018
16 Sun 2019
17 Stone 2013

The case can be made for all six:

Intermediary Role	Amazon's Activities
The Bridge	Amazon connects buyers and sellers who would not be able to find each other easily otherwise.
The Certifier	Amazon recommends certain products via prominent user reviews and search rankings, as well as the use of Amazon's Choice labeling.
The Enforcer	Amazon enforces the marketplace by adjudicating disputes and being able to kick bad actors off of its platform.
The Risk-Bearer	Amazon's strong brand and performance in other intermediary roles reduces the risk of online shopping for customers. As a distribution partner, Amazon shares some risk with merchants for poorly performing products. For both, Amazon handles credit card payments and therefore some financial risk.
The Concierge	Amazon's recommendations help customers decide on which products to buy, and their expertise with running an online marketplace helps merchants sell their products.
The Insulator	Amazon, in the case of dispute resolution, acts as an intermediary between buyers and sellers, keeping both at a professional distance from each other.

Its activities in each role reinforce each other. For example, by being an excellent Concierge, Amazon attracts more merchants to its site, which expands its presence as a Bridge.

Seeing how all of these roles are fulfilled is critical to evaluating what other goods and services Amazon can provide to its ever-growing list of customers.

As Amazon's founder and CEO Jeff Bezos has said, "If you don't understand the details of your business you are going to fail."[18]

---

18   Jopson 2012

KEY TAKEAWAYS

- Subsequent generations of digital intermediaries are disrupting existing digital intermediaries and differentiating themselves based on which roles they fulfill.

- Seeing these companies as mere "middlemen" doesn't do justice to the breadth and depth of the services they provide.

- Intermediaries can add serious value—and consequently command serious profits—by providing existing marketplaces with untapped Certifier, Enforcer, Risk-Bearer, Concierge, and Insulator services.

KEY QUESTIONS

- If your company is an intermediary, which roles is it currently filling?

- How can current customers understand and correctly value all of the intermediary services your company provides?

- Which unmet roles exist in your industry that could present an opportunity to assist customers via new services?

Chapter 4

WHAT'S NEXT

"Over the next 10 years, I expect many more industries to be disrupted by software, with new world-beating Silicon Valley companies doing the disruption..."

—MARC ANDREESSEN, CO-FOUNDER OF VENTURE CAPITAL FIRM ANDREESSEN HOROWITZ[1]

We have seen how reintermediation, fueled by the Digital Revolution, has been transforming both traditional and digital industries. First came the disruption of traditional intermediaries, such as the newspapers' "crown jewels" moving online either by their own accord or, more commonly, by new online players. This process continues, of course, with more and more aspects of commerce (e.g., retail shopping, banking, real estate) being wrenched into the digital world.

The second concurrent manifestation of reintermediation is early digital intermediaries facing new competition or complete supplantation by the next crop of

---

1   Andreessen 2011

intermediaries. Subsequent generations fulfill the same middleman roles better, or different roles entirely.

Cars.com, for example, is already 20 years old, which is an eternity for a technology company. Newer upstarts, such as Carsforsale.com (1999) TrueCar (2005), CarGurus (2006), LemonFree (2007), Carvana (2012), and Carsquare (2013), all angle for a piece of a similar pie. This type of competition is found in virtually any digital industry because the business opportunity is so large.

Much of entrepreneurship is focused exactly on these intermediaries. "The distinction between middlemen and entrepreneurs is rapidly blurring," says economist Michael C. Munger, "because improvements in the 'middleman' function - connecting buyers and sellers - are among the most fertile new spaces for entrepreneurial reimaginings."[2]

Traditional intermediaries are being replaced by digital ones; digital intermediaries are being disrupted by other digital intermediaries. So far, business-to-consumer (B2C) markets have been hit harder than business-to-business (B2B). And technology-centric industries have seen more disruption than sectors such as industrial.

"B2B has many more hurdles to adoption given the complex (and often offline) procurement processes," argues Bank of America analyst Justin Post.[3] But that is already

---

2   Munger 2018, 18
3   Sheetz 2019

beginning to change. Both B2B and industrial markets are facing more and more digital reintermediation.

"You know, tech spent many years eating itself... the [tech companies] that won out in the end were these really well-executing, super well-funded, tons-of-cash-flow machines," according to Ben Thompson, a prominent technology business analyst and author of the popular Stratechery newsletter.[4]

As the likes of Uber illustrate, digital companies are increasingly changing how physical goods and services are organized. Such firms are working furiously on embedding themselves in larger chunks of physical commerce and entering industries that aren't traditionally very digital at all.

Thompson sees blood in the water: "[A]ll these industries that used tech but were not fundamentally transformed by tech — they're just being mowed down. The carnage, I think, is going to be pretty epic when you get into broader industries."[5]

This is reinforced in the famous motto of leading venture capital firm Andreessen Horowitz, whose co-founder opened this chapter: "Software Is Eating the World."[6] And software is already nipping at the heels of traditionally non-digital industries.

---

4   "Ben Thompson On Business And Tech (Ep. 52)" 2018
5   Ibid.
6   "Andreessen Horowitz" 2019

DIGITAL AGRICULTURE

One industry in which I see these transformations through my consulting work is agricultural services. Companies in this area are increasingly figuring out how better to bring the advantages of technology to a very traditional industry. They know that if they don't take the lead, someone else will.

"We know that e-commerce will make inroads into B2B the way it has with B2C. We know that's going to happen, so we've got to develop capabilities now," says Lynn Guinn.

Guinn is the Global Strategic Pricing Leader for Commercial Excellence at Cargill, and he wrestles with the question of how the largest privately held U.S. corporation can keep itself relevant after over 150 years in business.

"What we really need to figure out is: how do we not let some outside computer junkie totally mess up our markets?" Guinn says, laughing.

Cargill is a massive conglomerate focusing on agricultural products and services, pharmaceuticals, financial services, and raw materials, among others. It earned just shy of $115 billion in revenue in 2018 and employs over 150,000 workers across the world. The Cargill family still owns over 90% of the company.[7]

Cargill may seem an unlikely candidate for high levels of innovation. Large and old companies tend to be

---

7   "America's Largest Private Companies" 2018

resistant to change, because change necessarily means moving away from what made the company large and old in the first place.

Leading photography film company Eastman Kodak couldn't keep up with the emergence of digital photography and declared bankruptcy in 2012. What is less known is that the first digital camera was actually created at Kodak. The company wasn't unaware of the technology, but it couldn't navigate how to balance its core business with such innovation. The resultant collapse has become a textbook case not of failure to innovate but of failure to adapt.[8]

To avoid a similar fate, Cargill is working hard to preempt reintermediation and disruption by others. "I don't want digital companies to be the only ones with money. The Guinn and Cargill families want to be rich, too," Guinn adds, smiling.

"The days of 'Hey, we're going to buy your crops, we're going to store it, we're going to play the carry'—you know, sell it at a profit—it's over," according to Cargill CEO David MacLennan.[9] He doesn't want Cargill to be the proverbial frog in slowly boiling water that doesn't realize its peril until it is too late.

Cargill's industries, of course, are not exempt from technology-fueled reintermediation. The trick for a company of

---

8   Anthony 2016
9   Parker and Blas 2018

Cargill's size and complexity is that digital reintermediation can come from so many different sides.

For instance, whereas it may have enjoyed a strong information advantage over competitors in the past, the internet has enabled anyone with a smartphone to access detailed data about commodity prices and weather forecasts. The storage and logistical capabilities of Cargill are also less valuable than they used to be, with farmers having many more options from which to choose.

So, it is incumbent on Cargill to leverage its strengths, such as deep customer knowledge and market experience, to play active defense and seek out new areas of growth. This involves keeping an eye on other companies that could reintermediate its industries.

Its efforts include investing in a satellite imaging startup, Descartes Labs, along with AI and machine learning to better predict crop patterns. Cargill could easily have bought such a company outright, but chose not to for strategic reasons. Not only does this allow Cargill to kick the tires and make sure such data analysis is valuable, but it also enables Descartes Labs to stay flexible as its own unit. Cargill's vice president and leader of global analytics James Weed's "main concern was that the tiny Descartes Labs would get lost within the bureaucracy of a giant company."[10]

---

10 Vanian 2018

Internally, Cargill invests heavily in software and skills training to stay on the cutting edge. Implementing new tools and processes in a large company is time-consuming and daunting, but the alternative is ossification and irrelevance.

"We're disruptors; we're disrupting our own industry," Guinn told me. "We never stop developing and we never stop advancing. As soon as you think you've got it figured out, you don't."

B2B AND INDUSTRIAL REINTERMEDIATION

Guinn and Cargill are right to be concerned about digital native companies entering their space and introducing new services. Technology giants that have honed their businesses in other industries could pose formidable challenges in B2B and industrial sectors.

In fact, that has already begun.

"[W]e're serving our customers by leveraging everything that's been built by Amazon and tailoring it to our business customers," says Martin Rohde, general manager of commercial customers at Amazon Business.[11]

Founded in 2015, Amazon Business is, as it sounds, the B2B arm of Amazon. Rohde explains the business unit:

---

11   Demery 2018

Amazon Business provides access to the hundreds of mil-lions of products available on Amazon.com. This includes everything from IT and lab equipment to education and food service supplies. Additionally, we provide access to more than 85,000 business sellers and we offer a list of business-only selection and pricing. For example, Amazon Business offers quantity discounts, which provides business customers the option to purchase in larger quantities.[12]

Amazon Business offers many tools to assist business customers with their procurement, including payment solutions, special tax exemptions, and heightened customer support.[13] It is focusing, therefore, on providing every intermediary role to B2B that it has already in B2C.

I became aware that Amazon Business had an eye on businesses adjacent to Cargill's agriculture specialties via a LinkedIn job posting delivered to me in early 2019.

"Amazon.com is looking for talented, driven and entrepreneurial people to focus on building our B2B product selection across the Tools and Lawn & Garden businesses," the job description read. Cargill (and Home Depot, Lowe's, etc.) should pay special attention to this "exciting

---

12   Ibid.
13   Post 2019

opportunity to work in the early stages of building the Tools and Lawn & Garden B2B business on Amazon."[14]

Amazon Business already has millions of customers, according to Bank of America analyst Justin Post:

In the past two years, [the gross merchandise volume] run rate has increased by 10 times: From $1 billion in 2016 to $10 billion in 2018, Bank of America said. And by 2023, the firm estimates Amazon Business can scale that gross merchandise volume run rate to $33.7 billion, with $16.1 billion in revenue.

Bank of America also believes that it's realistic to expect that by 2021 Amazon Business will capture 10 percent of the B2B market in the U.S. and 5 percent of the international B2B market. At that market reach, Bank of America said the unit would generate between $125 billion and $245 billion of added value for Amazon as a whole.[15]

Those are staggering numbers.

For the international B2B market, intermediaries that can offer Marina Krakovsky's Enforcer, Certifier, and Risk-Bearer roles will be especially valuable to customers. Many emerging markets have few existing political and market

---

14 "Amazon Business Sr. Vendor Manager: Tools And Agriculture" 2019

15 Sheetz 2019

institutions, in what is referred to as an *institutional void*.[16] This is an opportunity for private actors to provide additional services to entrants in these markets.

The scope of serving B2B and industrial sectors is enormous, and digital intermediaries want to get there before industry incumbents. As applications of information technology and digitization continue to grow at an astonishing pace, intermediaries will find newer and better ways to deliver value to customers.

BUT WAIT: WON'T BLOCKCHAIN KILL INTERMEDIARIES?

Thinking back to the beginning of this section, it is easy with hindsight to see how Gates and others' predictions of an intermediary-less digital economy were misguided. If anything, the process of reintermediation has only increased the importance of middlemen.

Today though, a new technology is reinvigorating the discussion around whether technology will make intermediaries irrelevant: blockchain.

Blockchain is, in simple terms, a distributed public ledger. "Distributed" means that it exists on thousands or millions of machines. "Public" means that anyone can view what has been recorded. A "ledger" is a record-keeping database. The mechanism by which the database or ledger

---

16   Gao et al. 2017

is updated makes it nearly impossible to hack or manipulate. This makes blockchain an excellent technology for
record-keeping, be it for contracts, transactions, or even
currencies such as bitcoin.[17]

A deep investigation of blockchain is outside of the
scope of this book, but armed with what we've learned in
this chapter, we are able to evaluate some of the claims
laid out by blockchain proponents about a disintermediated future.

Blockchain expert and co-founder of software company
Animal Ventures Bettina Warburg describes blockchain
technology for Wired in the following way: "Blockchain is
a new network, and it's going to help us decentralize trade,
allowing us to do a lot of our transactions much more
peer-to-peer directly and lower our use of intermediaries."[18]

Addressing how blockchain could be used to facilitate
transactions, she argues: "If we could guarantee the same
trade, using technology, as sort of a technological trust, we
wouldn't need all those middlemen in between."[19]

Warburg is hardly alone in this opinion. The *Harvard
Business Review* ran a piece in 2017 entitled "The Promise
of Blockchain Is a World Without Middlemen," claiming
that the technology represents "the promise of nearly

---

17 Fortney 2019
18 "Blockchain Expert Explains One Concept In 5 Levels Of Difficulty
    | WIRED" 2017
19 Ibid.

friction-free cooperation between members of complex networks... without central authorities and middle men."[20]

We can see that these examples are specifically addressing Krakovsky's Certifier and Enforcer intermediary roles. Having a nearly impenetrable and incorruptible record of transactions through blockchain will certainly be very valuable in some situations, such as in emerging markets as discussed earlier.

But blockchain enthusiasm runs the risk of ignoring what intermediaries actually do and customers actually want.

As Jose Arrieta, a senior U.S. government official with experience utilizing blockchain, said at a MIT-sponsored blockchain event: "The tech is cool, but if you're not driving value to the end user, what are you really doing?"[21]

Well, what do we know about what customers want from intermediaries? Certifier and Enforcer roles are only two of the six roles. While blockchain may have a substantial impact on those aspects, that is very different from saying that blockchain will eliminate middlemen. Certifier and Enforcer cover only a small amount of what customers find valuable in an intermediary.

From one point of view, a traditional bank may be an unnecessary intermediary, but from another it provides critical Risk-Bearing services to its customers. There is

---

20 Gupta 2017
21 Arrieta 2018

remedy when something bad happens. The fact that such financial services have proliferated is evidence that at least some customers find them very useful, and are implicitly willing to pay for them. Cryptocurrencies, built on blockchain, have risks that traditional financial services do not.

For example, losing your personal crypto key means you have absolutely no way of accessing your money. Krakovsky described this problem concisely: "The end result is very upset buyers with no way to access an asset they thought they owned." That is a big issue!

Such a scenario is a highly risky proposition for a method of transaction, let alone a long-term store of value. Customers may not want to accept all of that risk themselves.

"Something is lost when you completely distribute and decentralize all responsibility," Krakovsky argues.

In addition to forgetting one's personal key, another concern with blockchain-based cryptocurrency is theft. Stories of individuals and exchanges being hacked and losing millions of dollars make the news regularly. And this highlights another issue of such decentralized systems: little to no recourse in such situations.

"As a bank chief executive you can authorise a big wire transfer in a robbery, and then undo it the next day," explains Balaji Srinivasan, the CTO of Coinbase, an online platform for cryptocurrency trading. "Digital currencies are like handing over a suitcase of cash. You can't get it back."[22]

Traditional banking and credit providers aren't perfect for everyone, but they do have mechanisms to protect their users in the case of lost identification, theft, and fraud. Transfers often can be reversed. It is almost unbelievably easy to dispute a credit card charge. Banks can still collapse financially, but even then the government steps in with FDIC insurance (or may bail out the entire institution).

In addition to private key loss and theft, a third risk is personnel. The death of a key cryptocurrency exchange executive can put millions of dollars out of reach, as happened in late 2018, when cryptocurrency exchange QuadrigaCX's founder, Gerald Cotten, passed away suddenly.

"The laptop computer from which Gerry carried out the Companies' business is encrypted and I do not know the password or recovery key. Despite repeated and diligent searches, I have not been able to find them written down anywhere," said his widow.[23]

Being unable to find that key meant customers suddenly and irrevocably had no way of accessing their $190 million entrusted with QuadrigaCX. Such an organizational conundrum would be unthinkable with any traditional bank.

---

22 "A Disciplined Startup Emerges From The Wild West Of Crypto-Currency" 2018
23 Morris 2019

Like the bare-bones service from Craigslist, the flexibility and anonymity of blockchain is worth the risk for many people. But certainly not everyone. Many people want the value that intermediaries can provide.

As with the internet, blockchain will destroy some intermediaries but create the need for others. Reintermediation, not disintermediation.

Decentralized blockchain networks will surely change many industries, but so long as intermediaries provide additional value there will be customers willing to pay for it.

Thinking otherwise is to suffer from a very narrow view of the services such entities provide and fall prey to the same mistake as other technologists who thought the internet would bring disintermediation. Expect to see plenty of intermediaries popping up to facilitate blockchain and cryptocurrency technology as they grow.

* * *

Much how a forest fire clears out brush and dead trees to create space for new growth, digital disruption generates opportunities for new intermediaries to rise. The incredible growth we experience in information doesn't negate the need for intermediaries, but expands it.

Having too narrow a conception of what intermediaries do is a recipe for missed business opportunities. It is critical to think widely about the different roles that intermediaries can play in the marketplace and the various ways they create value.

Such investigation may uncover new opportunities or ventures, much how Scott Case recognized a particular gap in business travel intermediary services, leading to the founding of Upside. This analysis can also help your company play defense against being the target of reintermediation.

We can expect increased digitization only to accelerate the pace of reintermediation, churning industries and markets like whitewater. It is incumbent upon business leaders to be prepared, because the waters are only going to get wilder.

KEY TAKEAWAYS

- Reintermediation has been slower to interrupt B2B and industrial markets, but the process is well on its way.
- Incumbent B2B and industrial companies need a strategy in place to digitize and offer new forms of value to their customers.
- Even with new technologies like blockchain, intermediaries won't be disappearing anytime soon (and that's a good thing).

KEY QUESTIONS

- What will be the next predominantly physical industry to become reintermediated by digital players?
- How can incumbents balance the need to serve existing customers and existing services with the imperative to self-disrupt?
- What other upcoming technologies, rather than reducing intermediary options, actually provide additional opportunities to offer services to users and customers?

Part II

MONETIZATION

Chapter 5:

STATIC PRICES

"Price is a story. It is not an absolute number."

—*SETH GODIN, BUSINESS AUTHOR*

AND ENTREPRENEUR[1]

"If you went up to that chalkboard with prices on it and changed one number today, you'd add $25,000 to your bottom line this year," Scott Case of Priceline and Upside told the café owners.

As we saw in the previous section, Case knows a thing or two about pricing. As discussed, Priceline's key innovation was the *Name Your Own Price®* model that matched buyers and sellers in a new way. (The travel industry has long been innovative in the world of pricing, as we will continue to see.)

But for Case, one of the most interesting places to study the power of pricing is not in travel, but in small businesses. Why? Because so many small businesses rarely update their prices.

---

1   Ferriss 2018

"You walk into a deli, and you just know that the pricing hasn't been updated in a decade because the price board is printed in a way that it *couldn't* be updated," he told me.

And, as Case saw with one café, that can cost you tens of thousands of dollars a year in the sales of coffee alone.

* * *

The Digital Revolution has opened up new methods and models of pricing for every industry. We will examine these in the following chapters of this section. But the first step a modern business of any size needs to take is accepting that pricing is a verb, not a noun.

Too frequently, the price of a product or service is almost an afterthought for companies. If prices are updated at all, they are updated haphazardly without a clear strategy or analytical justification. While that may seem understandable for a small mom & pop business, in my consulting experience large corporations are just as guilty.

Price may seem a straightforward number, but for the most successful companies, it is anything but. The strategy that goes behind choosing different forms of pricing is intimately tied to how the company wants to position itself in relation to its competitors and its customers.

And the reality is that no company can afford to ignore its pricing strategy. There is no other lever that affects profitability as strongly as price. It pays to get it right, and getting it right requires continuous attention. Pricing is a verb.

Nothing in the modern economy can survive staying static. Critically, that includes pricing.

* * *

As I mentioned in the last chapter, Case worked on a startup that helped small businesses in between his time at Priceline and Upside. That startup, Main Street Genome, was the reason Case was talking to a couple Washington, D.C. café owners about their pricing.

Case was helping with a simple competitive price analysis. Comparing this café just to those within easy walking distance, Case found it was substantially underpriced. And in D.C., there are plenty of cafés nearby that want the same customers.

"The café was pricing their most commonly purchased item — a regular coffee — 50 to 60 cents less than anyone else in the neighborhood," Case told me.

The owners feared that raising price might cause them to lose customers. But Case calculated that simply raising its prices to the average for its surroundings would add a clean $25,000 a year to the café's bottom line, and he doubted that the lower price was retaining enough customers to offset that.

As a small operation with only two owners, this represented a substantial chunk of change being left on the table. Making such price changes would be easy, too. The only technological change would involve erasing the numbers on a chalkboard and writing them again. There wasn't even a point-of-sale system to update. Workers simply looked at the chalkboard to type in each item's price during a sale.

Seems like an easy decision. Yet, the owners hesitated to act for six months.

Raising prices seemed aggressive. When they finally did act, they did at half of Case's recommendation: instead of increasing by 60 cents to be just at the average of their nearby competition, they tacked on a mere 25 cents.

What the owners saw was what Case had predicted. They had no loss in volume. The café simply made more per cup sold. Those 25 cents were pure additional profit on every coffee sold.

In fact, in the first week after the price change, three customers *thanked* the café for raising its prices. These customers knew the café was underpriced and worried that it would go out of business. They were content, perhaps even happy, to pay more for a product that day than they had the previous week.

"Starbucks changes their pricing every 90 days at a minimum. If you're a café and you're competing with Starbucks, and they're evaluating their pricing constantly, and they're raising it three, four, six cents every quarter, that means they're raising their prices about 20 cents a year," Case explained.

"If you're competing with them, and your prices are stuck for three years, all of a sudden you're 60 cents a cup light. Which means you're not harvesting 60 cents in profit to either make your business better, subsidize a strategy you want to change, whatever it is," Case concluded. "You're screwed."

The café had *static prices*.

* * *

In my consulting work, it is not uncommon to find a company that hasn't updated its prices in over a year. Amazon, on the other hand, updates its prices on average every 10 minutes.[2] Companies that practice *dynamic pricing*, which we will investigate more in Chapter 8, can change prices literally every second.

With competitors like those, it is impossible for any company to keep its prices static for long. At Wiglaf Pricing, we work to establish teams and processes within organizations that span markets from software to industrial to ensure that their prices are up to date. The alternative is being quickly outpaced by changing competitive and market dynamics.

---

2   Mehta, Detroja and Agashe 2018

Yes, "menu costs," referring to the costs of communicating new pricing information, exist. But they are an insufficient justification for static prices, and in our digital world such costs are lower than ever. If a company is only making the occasional price change, then each change must be larger in degree and more noticeable to customers. By frequently updating its pricing, a company like Starbucks can make smaller and consequently less noticeable adjustments.

The Digital Revolution has made static prices particularly inexcusable, whether your company is a local café or a multinational heavy equipment manufacturer. The alternative is disastrous.

As business consultant and former CEO Katharine Paine puts it, "The moment you make a mistake in pricing, you're eating into your reputation or your profits."[3]

But updating prices regularly is only the first step organizations must take. In the rest of this Monetization section, we will investigate different pricing models and where they can work for your company.

KEY TAKEAWAYS

- Failing to regularly update your prices can be a substantial source of missed profits.

---

3   Meehan et al. 2011, 1

- Every company must accept that pricing isn't an occasional decision, but a continuous process. Pricing is a verb, not a noun.
- Keeping prices up-to-date vis a vis competition and market conditions is necessary but insufficient to defend profitability.

KEY QUESTIONS

- Does your company have processes in place to regularly assess its pricing?
- Who in your organization should be responsible for updating pricing?
- If your company's prices were out of line with the market, how would you know it?

Chapter 6

VARIABLE PRICING

*"Customers have different need states and life experiences.
Our aspiration is to exceed their expectations whatever
their need states might be."*

—*HOWARD SCHULTZ, FORMER CHAIRMAN
AND CEO OF STARBUCKS*[1]

A client of mine had a conundrum. As developers of a
revolutionary method to increase the speed and efficacy
of medical cellular testing, the company had to decide on
the best go-to-market strategy for bringing its product to
the market.

Creating better cellular testing conditions is valuable
primarily to two groups: research universities and pharmaceutical companies. The client didn't know which group
to target.

Pharmaceutical companies need to test their products
on cells, and my client's cell structures promised to save
researchers substantial time and money. The potential

---

1   Gapper 2011

value to a pharmaceutical company of a new breakthrough drug can be astronomical; increasing their odds of success even a little bit is worth a large amount of money. Such customers can afford to spend much more than a university for products that work.

Researchers at universities, on the other hand, face relatively modest budgets. They are seeking to make new scientific discoveries rather than create the next multi-billion-dollar drug. What they lack in funding, however, they make up for in prestige: high-level key opinion leaders (KOLs) who get good results with your products and publish in leading journals can be a boon for business.

The difference in willingness to pay between the two potential customer groups could be a factor of ten. My client wanted to know what price they should go to market with in light of such a large discrepancy. They knew the trade-offs they faced:

- If they priced high for the pharmaceutical companies, that price would effectively exclude most universities. They could miss the attention of KOLs who could demonstrate the effectiveness of their product and be an incredibly valuable user testimonial.

- If they priced low for the universities, however, they would be leaving a large amount of revenue and profit on the table. That money would be unavailable to cover the costs of research and production, reinvest in further development, and attract more investment.

Which group should they target? What price level should they introduce?

The tradeoff, in reality, was false. The best approach was to serve both.

* * *

When we consider buying a product, one of the questions we ask is: "What is the price?" When we are designing pricing strategies, however, the better question would be: "What are the *prices*?"

One of the first decisions a company must make in its pricing strategy is whether to offer different prices to different customers. Doing so is called *variable pricing*.

The alternative is *fixed pricing*. Fixed pricing entails every customer in every situation receiving the same price for the same product or service.

My client was coming from a fixed pricing point of view. I needed them to understand the benefits of variable pricing.

Fixed pricing is simple: one price for every customer. This is economically inefficient, however. As we saw with pharmaceutical companies and universities, different potential customers have a wide willingness to pay based on the value they get from a product.

Charging both groups of customers the same price doesn't match the different value that the product provides.

Either one group is priced out (e.g., universities with a high price), or the other group doesn't pay their fair share (e.g., pharmaceutical companies with a low price).

Potential customers have a wide range of willingness to pay, and so long as that willingness is higher than the marginal cost of providing the good, accepting the deal will leave your company better off, i.e., more profitable.

We can understand this graphically:

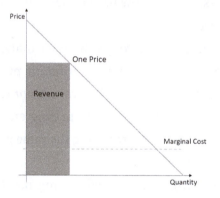

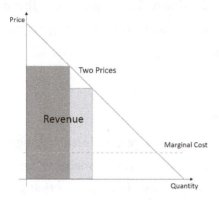

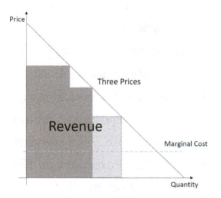

Adding price levels enables a company to earn more money and serve more customers. Grouping customers is called *customer segmentation*, and charging different amounts to these different groups is *price segmentation*.

Famed Harvard Business School professor Theodore Levitt once quipped: "If you're not thinking segments, you're not thinking."[2]

So, let's think.

PRICE SEGMENTATION

To go down the road of variable pricing, establishing good segmentation is critical. As we are segmenting for price, the segmentation should be done in a manner that groups customers into different buckets of willingness to pay. This method of segmenting the market and your customers is also referred to as a *segmentation hedge*.

Price segmentation is the result of recognizing that your customers are not a monolithic block. As we've seen, different customers (such as pharmaceutical companies and universities) have different purposes and willingness to pay for the same product or service. Price segmentation enables your company to capture customers at different profitable price levels, just like my client did.

As another example, senior citizens often enjoy special discounts due to their perceived tighter discretionary spending, willingness to shop around for a deal, and higher loyalty. A breakfast diner that offers such a discount may earn a loyal customer who comes in every morning for years to come. A movie theater that fills a seat at a

---

2   Levitt 1986, 128.

discounted senior rate while charging the regular rate for younger clientele can both serve more customers and earn higher profits.

From a value-based perspective, it makes complete sense to segment customers according to the different value they receive from a product or service. Both universities and pharmaceutical companies may be interested in your innovative new research product that enables better testing of new drugs. The university will be able to conduct better research and publish more papers. The pharmaceutical company, through better research, may be able to deliver a billion-dollar product to the market faster than before. While the university may gain prestige, the pharmaceutical company may gain enormous profits. The value to the pharmaceutical company, expressed in dollars, is much higher than the value to the university.

In the senior discount and university segment examples, you will notice the segments are clearly defined and hard to cheat. Either your appearance and ID indicate you are above a certain age, or they don't. Either your organization is a university, or it isn't. My client had several options for how to determine to which segment their prospective customers belonged.

There are risks with segmentation, though. If these categories aren't clearly defined and defensible, the segmentation may leak or completely fail. Too many customers may be able to claim the lower price despite the higher value, resulting in lost profits. Bad segmentation can be worse than no segmentation at all.

Also, any segmentation is at best an approximation of willingness to pay. For example, pricing movie theater tickets by age treats a 70-year-old pensioner and a 70-year-old CEO as the same despite very different incomes. Charging these two individuals the same price, from a willingness to pay segmentation perspective, is a missed opportunity.

(Even this example betrays an assumption: that a CEO would value a movie theater ticket higher than a pensioner. Perhaps the CEO doesn't care much for films, while the pensioner is an avid viewer of all the latest releases.)

Segmentation can only approximate individuals' willingness to pay and aggregate different preferences into one average. Individualized pricing, which we will discuss in Chapter 7, gets around this weakness, but has its own disadvantages.

METHODS OF PRICE SEGMENTATION

To create good segmentation, it is important to understand different segmentation methods. While there are many different ways to categorize such methods, I'll focus here on an arrangement based on the type of information that informs the grouping:

- Behavioral
- Demographic
- Blended (Behavioral and Demographic)

BEHAVIORAL

Customer behavioral-based price segmentation adjusts prices according to explicit rules regarding how customers behave.

Happy hours are a common example in some cities. Certain food and drink items are discounted for everyone during a certain time period, often right after work on a typically slow day (e.g., Tuesday).

Some merchants, such as gas stations, may charge you different amounts for paying by cash or credit card. The different prices are clearly listed and reflect to some degree the extra cost to the merchant of processing a credit card payment.

Business loyalty programs can also be thought of as a form of price segmentation if a long-time buyer receives a special discount due to their participation.

Such behavioral-based segmentation criteria are both *visible* and *non-exclusionary*.

Visible means the pricing mechanism is communicated to the customer. The purpose of a happy hour is to get customers to come, so customers must know about the happy hour in order to adjust their behavior. Customers know if they act a certain way (e.g., go during happy hour), they get a certain price (e.g., happy hour prices).

Non-exclusionary means, in theory, the special pricing is available to anyone who follows the prescribed rule. Customers know that certain prices (e.g., happy hour prices) are available to anyone who acts a certain way (e.g., goes during happy hour).

DEMOGRAPHIC

Behavioral-based price segmentation has to do with how the customer acts. Demographic-based segmentation, on the other hand, has to do with who the customer *is*. Let's look at a couple of examples.

Both a senior and university discount are demographic. Age, for better or worse, is an immutable part of who we are. Either an organization is a university or it isn't. Customers are sorted by who they are rather than how they act.

Some online services use location or billing zip codes to segment customers. Where someone lives can correlate with income and therefore willingness to pay, so such a sorting system can present customers in the same metro area with different prices. Where a customer lives is (largely) demographic. The goal is to match the price with willingness of the customer to pay, rather than identify any particular buying pattern. Aside from moving residences, a customer cannot change their behavior to get a different result.

In terms of visibility, you'll notice some demographic segmentation, such as a senior discount, may be advertised to the customer. Others, like zip code, almost certainly are not.

Demographic segmentation is exclusionary in intent: customers cannot easily change their segment.

BLENDED (BEHAVIORAL AND DEMOGRAPHIC)

There isn't a bright line separating behavioral segmentation from demographic segmentation. Some methods of customer segmentation and pricing share aspects with both. This is called *blended segmentation*.

Some online services will track your browsing history and use that information to adjust what price they display for a product or service. If you have looked at a certain product before, a system may determine you are already committed to buy and slightly increase the price. Or, a system may decide you're on the fence and need just a little discount to purchase.

In one sense, browsing history is a behavior. But this is a behavior being used for demographic ends: the goal is not to affect the customer's behavior, but to assess that customer's willingness to pay. Browsing history would not be used in a visible manner. This is a blended segmentation method.

As another example, let's consider a purely hypothetical pricing scheme where customers with iPhones are charged more for a product viewed via their mobile. The assumption here is that these customers have a higher willingness to pay than owners of other smartphone brands. One might argue customers could change their smartphone and therefore adjust their behavior to avoid the hypothetical surcharge. So, is this behavioral?

On the other hand, like the browsing history example, pricing via mobile device brand is not visible to the customer. Recall, behavioral pricing segmentation is explicit to the customer because one of the goals is to change customer behavior. We also know that the goal of charging by mobile platform would be to get at underlying characteristics of the person. Therefore, is such a scheme demographic?

These examples don't fit nicely into behavioral or demographic categorization. Therefore, they are blended.

(By the way, I'm just kidding about this example being hypothetical: travel intermediary Orbitz was caught serving Apple users costlier options than Windows users.)[3]

WHAT METHOD IS BEST?

Unfortunately, there's no easy answer to that. There are advantages and disadvantages to using behavioral and demographic characteristics to adjust your pricing and segment your market. One or the other is not "good" or "bad." Much can come down to notions of fairness.

A behavioral scheme, like a happy hour, is easy to understand, simple to implement, and widely accepted by customers. It can also, crucially, drive customer behavior in ways that are profitable to the merchant. The merchant

---

3   Mattioli 2012

wants more customers during the happy hour period; that is why the discount is being offered in the first place.

However, giving a blanket discount to everyone who walks into the bar at a certain time means many people who would buy at full price are not. The merchant is leaving money on the table.

A demographic approach, like a zip code scheme, is a bit harder to implement, but may give merchants a better approximation of willingness to pay. Therefore, they can collect more money from customers who don't mind while simultaneously offering discounts to other customers who otherwise would be priced out completely.

On the other hand, you may have felt a little uncomfortable reading about the zip code, browsing history, and device type segmentation in the demographic and blended sections above. As a customer, being secretly charged more simply because of who you are doesn't engender much brand loyalty to a company that acts in such a way.

Market norms are co-created between merchants and customers. These norms are different between industries and over time. Whereas most customers don't bat an eye at a senior discount, other demographic pricing can trigger deeply held feelings of injustice.

In an infamous example from 2012, it was found that Staples and other companies varied online prices based on zip code.[4] I already mentioned how Orbitz charged Apple users more than Windows users. Customers felt tricked. The companies received a lot of bad press.

There isn't one right answer, but it goes to show how tied up pricing strategy is with branding and larger corporate strategy. It takes careful planning to ensure that any price segmentation a company utilizes is in line with their other priorities.

CONSIDERATIONS

There is, of course, a trade-off in having variable pricing. The danger comes in that managing multiple prices is more difficult than one. Special care is required to:

- Establish fair price variance
- Communicate price variance
- Defend against segmentation leakage

ESTABLISH FAIR PRICING VARIANCE

Establishing a price variance which is understood to be fair is important if you want your customers to accept variable pricing. Your pricing strategy should help your customer relationship. The last thing you want to do is alienate potential customers through unfair price discrimination, as happened to Staples and Orbitz.

---

4   Valentino-DeVries, Singer-Vine and Soltani 2012

It is fair to charge a customer a higher price if that customer is more costly to serve, or to offer a discount to a customer who is less costly to serve, due to behavioral or demographic differences. It is generally seen as fair to charge customers different amounts based on the value that they receive, such as in our biotech example. It is not fair (or legal) to give a customer a favorable or less favorable price because of their race or religion.

COMMUNICATE PRICE VARIANCE

Communicating the price variance is critical in order for customers to accept that a price differential exists. And in the digital economy, there is no way to keep such variance secret even if it were in the company's best interest. From airlines to Amazon, we will see several examples of how variable pricing is done well and poorly.

If your discounts and rebates (together referred to as *commercial policy* or *price variance policy*) are intended to drive certain customer behaviors, then they must be communicated. Customers cannot adjust their behavior in response to an incentive if they don't know about the incentive!

DEFEND AGAINST SEGMENTATION LEAKAGE

Defending against segmentation leakage refers to the ability to clearly define and control who receives which price. For instance, if a lower cost-to-serve segment receives a lower price, but higher cost-to-serve customers are able to claim that lower price as well, your segments are leaking.

For my client, if pharmaceutical companies could easily pass themselves off as academic institutions and get a lower price, the segmentation would fail. There is however a clear divide between such organizations, therefore a reliable way to prevent leakage.

Pricing is an increasingly complicated world as technology transforms what is possible. The effects pricing decisions have on your customers can be subtle or explosive, so proceeding with caution and careful experimentation is important.

In terms of revenue and profit maximization, theory tells us that segmented pricing is better than fixed pricing. But this increased precision can come at a cost of perceived fairness and brand quality. A local café may know its regulars' differential willingness to pay, but it would be hard-pressed to offer different prices to a lawyer than to a non-profit worker. This would offend a sense of fairness.

Taking a stand against segmentation that is perceived as unfair can be a competitive advantage, as we will see in the case of Groupon in the next chapter. Providing a better customer experience through simplicity and fairness may offset the potential revenue advantages of segmentation.

BRAND CONSIDERATIONS

Apple, as one of the largest technology companies in the world, clearly has the capability to segment its customers. But variable pricing can connote a sense of lower quality if the focus for the customer becomes all about the price. Apple's branding is around its sophistication and high quality, therefore it has chosen to offer one price, take it or leave it.

"Apple doesn't do discounts," according to retail industry expert Barbara Farfan. "Apple has used a no-discount pricing strategy both with the products it sells in its own Apple retail stores and with the Apple products sold in all other retail chains like Wal-Mart and Best Buy."[5] The company wants to maintain the brand perception that its products are worth only a high price.

Priceline's matching model revolves around hotels offering discounts to travelers, but it doesn't show the specific hotel until the purchase has been made. This is similarly done to protect brand perception. Variable pricing can cut against a brand image that focuses on pure high-end quality.

There is a tradeoff in these different methods of pricing between precision and theory, fairness and simplicity. There is no answer that is right for every company.

---

5   Farfan 2018

The key question is how customers will react. In order to form a good hypothesis, a company must first aspire to understand its customers. Running small pricing experiments can test those hypotheses without betting the farm and being wrong. And collecting feedback from such experiments with customers becomes critical information to better inform pricing decisions going forward.

Above all, avoid a customer revolt.

KEY TAKEAWAYS

- Variable pricing through customer segmentation enables companies to serve more customers while earning higher profits.
- Successful customer segmentation requires carefully considered segmentation hedges and methods of separating customer groups.
- Variable pricing can cut against branding and other considerations, so it must be a strategic decision.

KEY QUESTIONS

- How do different groups of customers value your company's products and services differently from each other?
- What customers are you not currently serving who could be profitably served with better price variance policy?
- How does your company's price segmentation enhance profitability rather than leave money on the table?

Chapter 7

INDIVIDUALIZED PRICING

"The targeting of prices broadens the scope of who is able to pay and brings more people into the marketplace."

—PROFESSOR SANJOG MISRA, UNIVERSITY OF CHICAGO BOOTH SCHOOL OF BUSINESS[1]

If you understand now why multiple prices are more economically efficient and can drive higher profits than one price, you may have started wondering what the right number of segments is. In fact, wouldn't an unlimited number of segments and therefore unlimited number of prices be best?

---

1   Wallheimer 2018

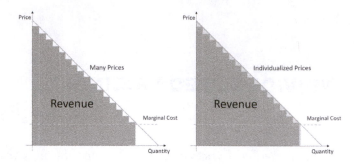

Theory tells us that yes, the more segments the better, so long as they are defensible. The logical result is segments that each contain a single customer. A segment of one.

Individualized pricing, also referred to as personalized pricing or customized pricing, treats each customer as a separate segment with its own price. For a solid individualized price, companies must be well informed regarding the customer's willingness to pay at any given time.

While this may seem like a major technological leap, in some ways individualized pricing is more of a return to what pricing was like for most of history.

LOOKING BACKWARDS

For most of human economic history, pricing was negotiation. If a potential customer walked into your shop or wanted to trade, you would have to make quick judgments about willingness to pay based off of attire, cleanliness, accent, confidence, etc.

Markets and retail in many parts of the world still feature this form of dynamic pricing. I have been woefully under-prepared for markets in Mexico, Morocco, Turkey, and China. In each situation, I have unsurprisingly been correctly identified having a higher willingness to pay being a foreign tourist than a local would have.

This was driven home especially hard at the Yungang Grottoes, an ancient complex of Buddhist temples and statuary carved from cliffs in China's Shanxi province. Visiting in 2008 during two months in the country, I tried to negotiate down the price of a bracelet from a local vendor outside the complex. She didn't budge, assuming correctly that for an already relatively inexpensive item, I was much less price sensitive than she was. Other nearby vendors smiled over my inexperience and quick capitulation to her price.

(I did have the baseline savviness to recognize the counterfeit bill she tried to give me as change: it was printed in black and white on common computer paper. I probably wasn't the first person she tried that on, so that trick must work sometimes!)

In a bazaar, bargaining works because the buyer and seller are able to assess each other face-to-face and make assumptions about each other's willingness to pay and willingness to accept. But as economies increase in sophistication, such interpersonal interactions are few and far between.

Fixed prices entered the modern business world when the scale and complexity of corporations and transactions made haggling a hassle. In an environment of short-term employees, variable costs, and heightened competition, the information and training cost for businesses became increasingly high. Additionally, as corporations became national brands and needed some level of uniformity across offices, the reputational cost of unfair pricing increased as well.

The price tag itself was invented in 1870 by two department stores, Wanamaker and Macy's. The growing needs of such stores involved exactly the training and branding requirements above. The price tag enabled salespeople to spend their time communicating product benefits and building a rapport with customers, rather than focusing on haggling over price.[2]

Today, in fact, it is typical for salespeople at companies not to know the cost or margin of the products they are selling. That is a common strategic and organizational decision especially when sales has the ability to negotiate price, a stark contrast to how commerce works in a bazaar of individual vendors.

A downside for customers of the modern but pre-digital economy has been that comparison shopping is difficult. In a bazaar, a customer can easily go from shop to shop.

2　"Episode 633: The Birth And Death Of The Price Tag" 2015

Doing so puts real time pressure on merchants' pricing. That is hard to do in the world of department stores.

For sellers, the pre-digital modern economy made it hard to know much about their customers. Customers were an anonymous mass, rather than individuals with known histories and preferences.

"Historically, [individualized pricing] has been very difficult to implement, mostly for logistical reasons," according to Harvard Business School professor John Gourville. But the Digital Revolution has upturned these difficulties. "With advances in technology and collecting of big data, then it may be that [individualized pricing] will become easier to do."[3]

As two-sided platform marketplaces like Priceline demonstrate, now we can have a plurality of buyers and sellers connected in real time. Both can negotiate essentially as if in a bazaar. Customers can comparison shop; sellers can personalize offers.

This can easily lead toward individualized pricing. In many ways, such a development is a return to the bazaar, this time aided by technology.

The price tag, when it exists at all, is written in pencil: adjustable and temporary.

---

3   Tanner 2014

A MODERN TAKE

Acceptance that customers each have a different willingness to pay naturally leads to individualized pricing. And technology is drastically reducing the historical costs of such pricing techniques.

Many software programs can make it easy to manage the pricing rules required to maintain dozens or even thousands of segmentation hedges. Data mining and statistical analysis has increased companies' ability to determine customers' willingness to pay.

Customer segmentation has often been a more efficient approximation of individual willingness to pay, but today that assumption is substantially weaker. And customers are coming around to the idea that the price one person sees online may be different than what another sees, or what that same person sees five minutes later.

The enormous success of technology companies with complex pricing, such as Amazon and Uber, both from a customer satisfaction and a pricing strategy perspective, is a testament to this. Many other companies are exploring ways that they can take advantage of similar resources to implement individualized pricing.

Individualized pricing requires reams of data, strong technological support, and skilled practitioners to maximize profitability. These resources are not insubstantial. It should come as no surprise then that companies leading the way with individualized pricing are tech-native.

I came across one such company in Washington, D.C.

"The key task for us is creating the minimum discount needed to pull in a diner and the maximum discount needed to get the diner off the couch," Cherian Thomas told me.

Thomas is the co-founder and CEO of Spotluck, a service that offers discounts at local restaurants. While the idea to help restaurants attract new customers via discounts certainly isn't novel, Spotluck's approach to the problem is.

"Prices in a restaurant on a Tuesday at 2pm when it's raining shouldn't be the same as prices in a restaurant on a Friday night at 6 when it's beautiful out," Thomas explained.

"I wanted to see whether I could fix the problem of restaurants being hesitant to vary their prices." Thomas started working on Spotluck while at Georgetown University and founded the company in 2014 to answer that question.

Spotluck is a mobile app that, with the spin of a digital wheel, reveals special discounts to a number of eateries in your area. The gamifying aspect of spinning a wheel is entertaining, but also introduces some randomization in what discount level and to which eatery the user receives.

Spotluck is in the game of segmenting a restaurant's potential customers and determining what their willingness to pay is at the moment they use the app. By individualizing the discount shown and seeing whether it prompts action, Spotluck is able to hone in on the optimal discount to motivate new sales.

With a dig at some of the earlier players in the space, Thomas said, "We've proven that you do not need to give a 50% discount and take 50% of the revenue to move somebody on a Tuesday."

I witnessed Spotluck's weather-based pricing mechanism in action one March in Washington, D.C. I was supposed to be on a quick morning flight to New York City to see a client, but a blizzard hit the Mid-Atlantic, shutting down runways and grounding planes. I was instead at Union Station, hoping against hope that trains would still be running.

My pocket vibrated with an alert from Spotluck, and I saw a special discount had been activated. The snow had shut down most transportation, but dining establishments still wanted to serve customers. While the weather was unkind, many people probably still wanted to eat. A special discount could entice those people to go out to eat even with the weather dampening demand.

I still had to figure out how to get to New York City, so I didn't act on the discount. But a user not acting is still useful information to Spotluck and its merchants. It suggests the presented discount wasn't enough to motivate action. Such a data point becomes an input for next time.

Since Spotluck can tie the user to a specific discount at a specific eatery, among many other variables, it can develop a picture of what exactly it takes to motivate an individual customer to action. Restaurants can accurately assess the effect of the app on its business because the discounts are only visible through the app.

Such targeted pricing and segmentation makes the value Spotluck provides clear, while giving its merchants greater control over their promotions than they could get from any traditional advertising.

DECLINING THE OPTION

While the power of individualized pricing is undeniable, companies must determine whether such a strategy makes sense for them. The answer to that is not a foregone conclusion.

A company like e-commerce giant Groupon has detailed customer profile data, the ability to run experiments on millions of transactions across hundreds of regions, and the flexibility to adjust prices on a moment's notice. It may be surprising, therefore, to learn that Groupon has decided *not* to practice individualized pricing.

"We could charge customers different prices, but we've decided that's the route to a bad customer experience," explained Jason Pearcy, at the time a senior pricing and data scientist at Groupon. "We don't want to charge you one price and charge someone else a random price just based on different browser histories."

As mentioned earlier, I worked at Groupon for a couple years starting in 2011, starting right before the company went public. My role involved sales and marketing analysis, and it was fascinating to see how the company was constantly adjusting its value proposition to find out what stuck best for merchants and customers alike. The technology for determining which deals to feature on the site and who should receive what offers in their email steadily improved during my two years there.

Working now in pricing strategy and circling back for this book, I was excited to learn how Groupon is utilizing its technology for pricing. I didn't expect to find an example of a technology company bucking the trend against individualized pricing. At least for core Daily Deals, the price one customer sees is the same as the next. Despite the capability to do so, Groupon plays no games with individualized pricing.

That wasn't a foregone conclusion. When Pearcy joined in 2016, the team was developing the capability to make individualized pricing happen. But they took a step back. "We decided to think hard and carefully about what we wanted to do," Pearcy told me.

Pearcy was a strong advocate against individualized pricing, despite knowing they could develop the technical ability to enact it. For him, it comes back to the customer experience, and "customers get really pissed off if you charge them different prices just based on who they are," he says. We saw some examples of this in the previous chapter, Variable Pricing.

Of course, a company with the geographical reach and technological backbone of Groupon isn't sitting on its hands when it comes to pricing strategy and determining the right price for different offerings. The fact that the company occasionally offers promotional codes is evidence that it does vary price. The company has simply decided that using individualized pricing is not an appropriate tool, given its priorities.

"We're going to focus on targeting what the right price is, rather than experimenting on individual users. We want to figure out which deals are overpriced and adjust them downward, and figure out which are underpriced and adjust them upward," Pearcy told me. "We're taking a data-driven approach to the prices we offer every day."

PROCEED WITH CAUTION

Fairness is a tricky subject. Notions of fairness are contingent on culture and malleable across time. Many customers were upset when airlines started variable pricing, but have come to accept it. Why with airlines and hospitality but not other industries?

In June of 2017, Uber admitted to experimenting with individualized pricing.[4] Uber would have preferred

---

4   Kukura 2017

its individualized pricing experiments to remain private. Why? Customers don't like feeling cheated.

Uber tried to control the narrative. "We price routes differently based on our understanding of riders' choices so we can serve more people in more places at fares they can afford," according to a spokesman.[5] But customers didn't buy it.

Business consultant Rafi Mohammed shares a story in which he noticed that he was seeing a different price for a vacation package in Orbitz's app versus Orbitz's website. The exact same package was 6.5% more via the website.[6]

He then did a test with the friend he was with. The price she saw in her Orbitz app was 2.8% more than his for the exact same deal.

"Amazingly," writes Mohammed, "Orbitz knew something that I regularly give my friend good-natured grief about: She overpays for almost everything."[7]

Something similar has probably occurred to most readers. And getting charged more than your friend typically doesn't feel very good. Orbitz, for its part, said the price difference must have been due to an A/B test or some pricing anomaly.

"The bottom line, though, is that... a rudimentary type of personalized pricing is occurring: Some customers

---

5   Ibid.
6   Mohammed 2017
7   Ibid.

are receiving different prices than others," according to Mohammed.[8]

* * *

A study by researchers at Seattle University revealed profit was maximized in an experiment with individualized prices, as were measures of consumer satisfaction and welfare. In their setup, participants were able to name their highest willingness to pay for a slice of pizza delivered at the end of class. That willingness to pay, in short, was used to price the service for each individual, giving everyone "the opportunity to purchase at what is believed to be a fair price."[9]

The study also found, however, consumer satisfaction and assessment of fairness collapsed when participants were informed of how their individual preferences were used to derive individualized prices.

"Despite ratings of satisfaction, once [participants] learned that they had been given different prices for the same product, a large majority were clamorous and in agreement in their condemnation of customized [individualized] pricing," the researchers reported. "Even some

---

8   Ibid.
9   Obermiller, Arnesen and Cohen 2012

who had paid less than their [willingness to pay] raised objections."[10]

That last statement is remarkable. If a customer has willingness to pay of five dollars and is charged four dollars, theory tells us that person should have one dollar of consumer surplus. Any consumer surplus, by definition, makes the consumer better off than before.

What this study suggests is that simply *knowing how a product was priced* can turn an economically beneficial transaction into a strongly unpleasant experience.

The authors conclude that "given consumer expectations of standardized pricing, differences in price across consumers are considered unfair, but when consumers expect customized pricing, those same price differences are not perceived as unfair."[11]

This should give pause to companies who want to experiment with individualized prices.

A different study at the University of Pennsylvania found deep discontent with the idea of individualized prices. A sample of their findings include:

- 76% of respondents agreeing that "it would bother me to learn that other people pay less than I do for the same products"

---

10   Ibid.
11   Ibid.

- 87% of respondents disagreeing that "it's OK if an online store I use charges people different prices for the same products during the same hour"
- 84% of respondents agreeing that "websites should be required to let customers know if they vary charges for the same items during the same period"[12]

Customers of course would prefer to pay less than their highest willingness to pay, and no one likes to be a sucker, so such findings shouldn't be shocking. But they are worth serious consideration as to how best to practice and communicate variable pricing, let alone individualized pricing.

* * *

"Personalised pricing is... problematic," says Ariel Ezrachi, author and law professor at the University of Oxford. "It's based on asymmetricity of information; it's only possible because the shopper doesn't know what information the seller has about them, and because the seller is able to create an environment where the shopper believes they are seeing the market price."[13]

In 2000, customers discovered that Amazon was charging different people different amounts. The fallout was great enough for founder and CEO Jeff Bezos to

---

12   Turow, Feldman and Meltzer 2005
13   Walker 2017

promise that such pricing discrepancies were simply randomized tests.[14] Customers felt cheated.

Another downside of individualized pricing: it can't be used to guide customer behavior. Recall from Chapter 6: Variable Pricing that one of the benefits of using clear, communicated behavioral characteristics to segment is that customers can tell which of their behaviors are costly. If there is a 3% surcharge for shipping, a customer can decide whether that 3% is worth saving by picking a product up from the warehouse. The amount of customers who choose shipping vs. pickup then informs the company about its own customers' preferences.

But if a customer is getting an individualized price via an opaque pricing process, they are not being told how their behavior may affect that price. In turn, the company may be missing out on useful information, as in the shipping vs. pickup example above. This is similar to the opacity and disadvantages present in many demographic segmentations schemes.

Too much emphasis on behavioral customer characteristics has a potential downside as well: it may invite customers to game the system. A common successful technique for getting a discount while online shopping is to put a desired product in the shopping cart... then leave. Many merchants will send a promotion to influence customers to

---

14   Borison 2015

move from the shopping cart to the purchase button. Too heavily a reliance on behavioral characteristics therefore might encourage enough subterfuge to render individualized pricing an expensive effort at turning off customers.

With individualized pricing, largely speaking, you are who you are. You can't change purchase behavior to get a better price, nor can you change your demographics. Consequently, as a business, you cannot use price segmentation to encourage your customers to act in ways that are more profitable to you as well.

For what it is worth, Amazon has moved away from individualized pricing experiments itself.

"Our customers expect to come to Amazon and find the lowest prices across our vast selection," Amazon spokesperson Scott Stanzel said, explaining that all customers see the same prices. "So we are doing the hard work for them. Amazon scours prices - both offline and online - in order to make sure we meet or beat the lowest prices out there."[15]

As a baseline, companies must have substantial resources to consider individualized pricing. Such pricing still requires careful consideration of how customers will react in order to decide whether this is an appropriate model to implement.

---

15   Ibid.

KEY TAKEAWAYS

- Individualized pricing is the result of shrinking customer segments down to a single individual.
- Done well, individualized pricing maximizes profitability by charging every customer a tailored price.
- Individualized pricing carries risks though, and simply having the technological capability to implement it doesn't make it the right strategic choice.

KEY QUESTIONS

- Does your company have the information technology capability to consider individualized pricing?
- Is individualized pricing aligned with your company's other strategic priorities and values?
- How would you manage your customers' reactions if you were to implement individualized pricing?

Chapter 8

DYNAMIC PRICING

"[Dynamic pricing] is not a matter of stealing more money from your customer. It's about making margin on people who don't care, and giving away margin to people who do care."

—ULRIK BLICHFELDT, CEO OF PRICING
SOFTWARE COMPANY A2I SYSTEMS A/S[1]

M. Douglas Ivester, CEO of Coca-Cola in the late 1990s, was frustrated. The rules of economics state that when the demand of a product is high or supply is low, the price of that product should increase. Why couldn't he do that with his prices?

Airlines and hotels, for instance, had been doing so for years. Typically, the closer to the date of travel, the lower the supply of seats and beds, and therefore the higher the price. Customers who purchase a flight with just a few days' or hours' notice probably need it more too, and therefore value it higher.

---

1   Schechner 2017

Ivester wanted to apply that thinking to his industry. On a hot summer day, customers value Coke more. "So, it is fair that it should be more expensive," he said.[2]

In 1999, he had the opportunity to test this hypothesis. That year the company began testing a "smart" vending machine that could automatically raise prices in warm weather.

Executives at Coke were thrilled. They had the opportunity to bring *dynamic pricing* to an entirely new category.

* * *

Dynamic pricing refers to market pricing that is flexible and timely according to supply and demand. When demand is high or supply is low, prices increase. Conversely, prices decrease when demand is low or supply is high.

The Digital Revolution has created companies that are better able than ever to practice such pricing strategies. Ride-hailing companies, such as Lyft and Uber, are some of the best known to offer a different price for the same product (i.e., a given route) every time a customer opens the app.

At periods of high demand or low supply, the price of a ride increases. This is meant to encourage more drivers to get on the road and discourage more price sensitive

_____

2   Hays 1999

riders from taking a trip. Conversely, prices decrease when demand is low or the supply of drivers is too high. Potential riders may then choose Uber over alternate transportation options, and drivers may move to an area of higher demand or take a break.

Amazon is emblematic of dynamic pricing for physical goods, changing product prices 2.5 million times a day according to demand, competitors' prices, and inventory, to name a few factors.[3]

WHAT DYNAMIC PRICING ISN'T

Dynamic pricing is commonly associated with *variable pricing*, a concept discussed in the previous chapter, but is actually quite different. While variable pricing refers to offering different groups of customers different prices at the same time (i.e., price segmentation), dynamic pricing specifies changing price *over time.*

A company's pricing could be fixed across customers but flexible with supply and demand, demonstrating dynamic pricing but not variable pricing. This is what Coke wanted to try: charging all customers the same dynamic price. Conversely, a company could have multiple customer segments but keep prices static for months at a time, such as a movie theater.

---

3   Mehta, Detroja and Agashe 2018

Dynamic pricing describes an axis of *time*. Variable pricing describes an axis of *segmentation*. It is possible to have one without the other.

Dynamic pricing is also frequently associated with *revenue management*, but once again is separate. Revenue management is best thought of as a subcategory of dynamic pricing.

Revenue management, referred to in Chapter 2: Innovating on Traditional Intermediaries, refers to pricing techniques used when supply is limited and expires after a certain time period. It originated in the airline industry, where you cannot simply add additional seats to a flight, and once the flight takes off, any empty seats have zero value. From there it has spread into other industries with similar dynamics, including hospitality and events ticketing. In those industries, similarly, the value of an empty hotel room or a vacant seat goes to zero if they aren't filled.

Dynamic pricing doesn't require limited supply or expiration. It is a wider concept.

Using Uber as an example, one of the stated goals of increasing prices during periods of high demand is to encourage more drivers to become available, thus increasing supply. Airlines, hotels, and performance venues cannot simply add capacity. They are solving a slightly different problem. Revenue management is a specific form of dynamic pricing, but not all dynamic pricing is revenue management.

Sometimes the example of grocery stores discounting goods that are close to expiration is used as an example of dynamic pricing. However, dynamic pricing properly describes a much more active practice. Recall, dynamic pricing must be flexible and time-limited. The price of a browning banana is only flexible in one direction: down.

Contrast that to Uber constantly shifting price (both up and down) and the difference in approach and sophistication becomes apparent.

"Uber's base fares are typically less than a taxi, but when a baseball game lets out and demand spikes, prices go up," explains Alex Shartsis, the CEO of Perfect Price, a software company that applies AI to pricing. "You may have to pay more, but you can always get a car when you need one -- and more drivers show up at the ballpark knowing there are better fares. As people leave and availability opens up again, the price goes back down."[4]

What we end up with is a pricing categorization that looks like this:

---

4   Shartsis 2019

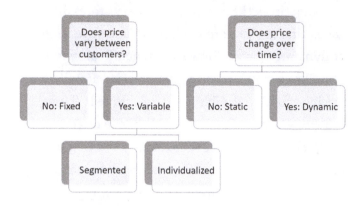

DYNAMIC PRICING CONSIDERATIONS

Now that we better understand what dynamic pricing is, we can analyze what it requires to be successful.

Dynamic pricing done right at a technical level requires powerful information technology. Since technology makes both the inputs and outputs of dynamic pricing easier to manage, we've seen a large increase in its use with increased digitization.

But the technical issues are only part of successful dynamic pricing. More important is the same concern that lurks behind individualized pricing: will customers accept it?

This is largely a cultural question.

Customers have become accustomed to the idea of dynamic pricing in certain industries. As mentioned, airlines and hotels were among the first. Uber and its contemporaries have proved that customers are willing to have dynamic pricing in local transportation, but not without difficulty.

Uber goes through great pains to communicate and explain its pricing to customers, publishing numerous articles with titles like "How Uber's dynamic pricing model works,"[5] "What is dynamic pricing?"[6] and "Why are prices higher than normal?"[7] Such communication is critical to getting customers to accept this pricing strategy.

It is important to note too that Uber's method of communicating its dynamic pricing has changed substantially over time in an effort to best engage its customers. We will take a closer look at Uber's pricing communication development in our Transparency revolution.

But companies in other industries have fallen flat despite the appealing logic behind dynamic pricing. Bars and restaurants that apply such pricing are few and far between. The vast majority of movie theaters don't increase the price of their tickets as showtime approaches, despite that being a clear opportunity for revenue management.

Why? Customers recoil from the idea. "Whether it's a nickel or a dollar, people have a way of getting used to their prices," according to NPR's Planet Money.[8]

---

5   "How Uber's Dynamic Pricing Model Works" 2019
6   "What Is Dynamic Pricing?" 2019
7   "Why Are Prices Higher Than Normal?" 2019
8   "Why The Price Of Coca-Cola Didn't Change For 70 Years | Planet Money | NPR" 2018

Village Cinemas, an Australian chain, ended its experimentation with dynamic pricing weeks earlier than intended due to customers' outcry. It had attempted to adjust its concession pricing upward during times of higher demand, but customers felt cheated.[9] Given that concessions can generate margins as high as 85%, it is understandable that cinemas would want to optimize their pricing.[10] But it was a communication failure. Customers accused the company of "price gouging."[11]

Regal Cinemas, meanwhile, is running its own experiments with dynamically pricing its movie tickets.[12] Will they find more success than Village Cinemas or run into the same problems?

The promise for companies who figure out how to bring it to their industries is real, but so is the peril. Companies "should look at this more strategically," according to Aloke Mondkar, retail pricing expert. "What are my customers telling me? Is this aligned with what my customers are willing to accept? Is it relevant to the business I'm in?"[13]

These are important questions for any company to answer. In the end, it's for customers to decide.

---

9   Fussell 2018
10   Morris 2017
11   Fussell 2018
12   Hayes 2017
13   Bhattacharyya 2019

* * *

You might be wondering what happened with Coke's experimentation. Unfortunately, their outcome was similar to that of Village Cinemas.

Customers hated the idea, referring to the company's attempts to dynamically price as "gouging," the same language Village Cinemas' customers had used. The shock of paying more for a cold drink on a hot day was too much. According to the *New York Times*, "Coke responded by running away from the heat-seeking vending machine as fast as possible."[14]

Companies must proceed with caution despite the hype around dynamic pricing. A misstep can create the opportunity for competitors, correctly or not, to reaffirm their commitment to "fair" pricing. In the case of dynamically priced vending machines, chief rival Pepsi took advantage of Coke's mistake to clarify its own position:

"We believe that machines that raise prices in hot weather exploit consumers who live in warm climates," declared Pepsi spokesman Jeff Brown. "At Pepsi, we are focused on innovations that make it easier for consumers to buy a soft drink, not harder."[15]

Being an industry leader in dynamic pricing is an opportunity, but success depends on the right data,

---

14 Leonhardt 2005
15 Hays 1999

technology, products, and customer communication. It also must align with larger company strategy. Customers' notions of fairness are deeply ingrained yet hard for them to articulate beforehand.

Nonetheless, the promise of better inventory management and higher profitability for companies, combined with uneven but increasing customer comfort with changing prices, means that dynamic pricing will continue to make inroads. It is incumbent on companies to determine their strategy to prepare.

KEY TAKEAWAYS

- Dynamic pricing refers to changing price over time in accordance with supply and demand.
- Digital technology has made dynamic pricing easier for more and more companies, but customer expectations remain major hurdles that require careful management.
- Contrary to hype, dynamic pricing should not be the desired strategy for every company or industry.

KEY QUESTIONS

- Does your company have the data and technological capabilities, as well as the industry dynamics, to consider dynamic pricing?
- What is your customer communication plan for enacting dynamic pricing?

- Is there an opportunity for your company to differentiate itself by *not* dynamically pricing?

Chapter 9

SUBSCRIPTION AND METERED PRICING

"Every day that passes, Apple cares less about how many iPhones they ship, and more about how many Apple ID's they can gather, and how much revenue they can generate per ID."

—TIEN TZUO, FOUNDER AND CEO OF ENTERPRISE
SOFTWARE COMPANY ZUORA[1]

"How did I just spend *$60* at CVS?" Perfect Price's Alex Shartsis wondered. "Oh, I bought some razors."

His frustration at the price of shaving razors at traditional retailers is a common one. A simple and small piece of metal is often one of the most expensive personal care items regularly purchased by both men and women.

The fact that razors seem more expensive than they ought to be has occurred to many consumers. The

---

1   Whitler 2016

differential value between one razor and another, objectively, must be rather low. They're little pieces of metal.

In fact, the so-called razor-razorblade model of pricing had become a standard business school example of selling one item near cost (the razor handle) while charging high margins on the disposable (the blade). King C. Gillette, the eponymous founder of the leading razor company, summed it up as "give 'em the razor; sell 'em the blades."[2]

Manufacturers attempt to "shroud" the cost of disposable add-ons, such as razors and printer ink. One study found that only 3% of printer owners knew the cost of their printer's ink when they purchased it.[3]

In 2012, Gillette's company represented 72% of the U.S. razor market, which was valued at billions of dollars.[4] Insider information on its margins suggested that its price mark-up could top 4,000%.[5] Indefensibly high prices and suspected juicy margins can place quite a target on a company and its industry.

"As a pricing guy," Shartsis says, "it seems apparent that if you're selling a piece of aluminum that costs pennies to manufacture but charging $60 for it, somebody's going to come up with a way to manufacture the same thing for the same cost and charge much less."

---

2 "How Food And Beverage Companies Save On Film And Paper Banding" 2015
3 Gabaix and Laibson 2006
4 Trop 2017
5 Poulter 2009

And that's exactly what a company called Dollar Shave Club did.

SUBSCRIPTION MODELS

How can a company compete in an established industry without a revolutionary new product? One option is by overturning pricing assumptions. In Dollar Shave Club's case, that meant selling razors via a low monthly subscription rate.

Dollar Shave Club doesn't make its own razors. They are rebranded Dorco razors, which customers could also buy through sites such as Amazon or directly from the manufacturer.[6] Therefore, the company properly represents a new intermediary in the razor market. Dollar Shave Club is simply a new way to buy. Its innovation is purely its pricing model.

Subscriptions make sense for razor blades because they encourage regular consumption and customer lock-in. And the simplicity of its offering appealed to customers who wanted the convenience of a subscription. It therefore represented a double threat to traditional razor sales: lower price and higher convenience.

In 2012, Dollar Shave Club had revenue of $4 million. In 2013, $19 millon. In 2014, $65 million. Revenue surpassed $100 million in 2015.[7] Dollar Shave Club was acquired by

6 Wolff-Mann 2016
7 Lashinsky 2015

Unilever, one of Gillette's main competitors, for one billion dollars in 2016.[8]

That's quite the four-year accomplishment for a company selling small pieces of metal in a heavily serviced market.

Dollar Shave Club razors perhaps weren't amazing, but they were certainly good enough for their large target market. If a customer doesn't recognize the extra value of a deluxe Gillette razor, that value doesn't exist, and therefore neither can a premium price. Customers were hungry for an alternative.

"There's kind of a game going on, where there's way too much margin," said David Pakman, a venture capitalist who invested in Dollar Shave Club. "The big guys are overcharging you, while smaller companies like [Dollar Shave Club] can give you the best products in the world for a fraction of the price."[9]

* * *

Such a strategy and rapid growth would have been next to impossible before the Digital Revolution. From 2011 to 2016, e-commerce subscription services revenue

---

8   Cao and Mittelman 2016
9   Isaac 2014

grew from $57 million to $2.6 billion, a growth of 100% every year.[10]

One of the most common examples is software-as-a-service (SaaS), in which software is sold and hosted as a subscription rather than a single purchase and install. Salesforce, makers of customer-relationship management (CRM) software, is one of the most prominent SaaS providers with over $13 billion in revenue in 2018.[11]

Established software suppliers have taken notice. Microsoft Office, once sold as a single install, is now most popular in its subscription Office 365 format, with over 200 million consumer and business users at the beginning of 2019.[12] Microsoft has "brilliantly navigated" this transition, according to Stratechery's Ben Thompson, being "remarkably well-placed to take advantage of this new paradigm."[13]

"Today, companies are less concerned about the number of units shipped than they are about the successful outcomes they deliver and the consistent, positive interactions they have with each and every one of their customers," says Tien Tzuo, CEO of Zuora, an enterprise software company that helps companies manage their own subscription-based services.[14]

---

10   Chen et al. 2018
11   Trefis Team 2019
12   Protalinski 2019
13   Thompson 2019
14   Whitler 2016

Transforming business models from a single purchase to recurring subscription revenue isn't easy. But the promise is high. At Wiglaf Pricing, we've assisted several software companies with the transition. With the right setup, subscription pricing can be far more profitable for companies while better aligning value-delivery incentives with the customer.

"The brilliance of paying on a subscription basis is that a company can buy exactly what it needs, when it needs it, and no more," says Thompson.[15] This opens up products to many new customers who couldn't previously afford a high one-time purchase. In this sense, subscriptions can open up new customer segments just like variable pricing can.

A subscription can also be a way to engender customer loyalty. Through repeated exposure and experience, a customer becomes habituated to engagement with the company. The customer tends to consider the average value received too, rather than the value of each unit: few magazine subscribers cancel their account if one particular issue is less interesting than the magazine is generally, for example.

The flipside is that successful subscription models depend on keeping the customer a customer. Lifetime valuations and customer experience increase in importance

---

15   Thompson 2019

when the seller must continuously demonstrate the worth of its products and services.

Already the pricing model innovator, Uber is testing monthly subscription plans for riders in some cities.[16] Given that ride-hailing customers care mainly about getting from point A to point B rather than the app that arranges the ride, such pricing model experimentation may be a way for Uber to encourage greater loyalty and lock in riders.

HARDWARE SUBSCRIPTIONS

Technology has also enabled many more industries to investigate subscription pricing. Such models, thanks to digitization, are increasingly being adopted in industrial settings, as well. Subscriptions are a way to price based on the value a machine actually provides and a method by which to rent expensive hardware.

Hardware has lagged behind software for subscription models in large part due to its physical nature. Someone must move, store, maintain, and service hardware. But digitization is reducing these costs, and businesses used to one idea of ownership are changing.

"[Q]uite frankly, our culture as a whole has become more comfortable with the idea of renting versus buying," says Matt McLean, product manager at Volvo Construction

---

16   "Self-Driving Cars Will Require New Business Models" 2018

Equipment. "I think we will continue to see an upward trend in rental."[17]

Many automotive manufacturers offer subscription programs to access their vehicles. For example, "Book by Cadillac" was a subscription service begun in 2017 whereby Cadillac customers could swap in and out of different vehicles for a flat $1,800 monthly fee. It was paused in 2018 due to higher than anticipated costs and logistical issues, but the promise was there.[18]

A new version, "Book 2.0," is anticipated to launch in 2019, this time with closer collaboration with dealers on operations, service, and maintenance.[19] (We will investigate the relationship between manufacturers and dealerships more in the Channel revolution.) With such programs, customers can enjoy multiple vehicles without paying tens of thousands of dollars upfront.

This is one big advantage of subscription programs: they lower the barriers to entry for customers. Companies no longer need to pay millions for a large industrial capital expenditures; consumers pay tens of dollars a month for software services rather than hundreds or thousands up front.

---

17   Association of Equipment Manufacturers 2019
18   Dellinger 2018
19   Wayland 2019

One investment fund created to help bring subscription models out of the software world and into the hardware space is Baseline Growth Capital.

"We're doing for hardware what SaaS did for software," founders Joel Gheen and Raghav Mathur explained to me over coffee in Denver's Cherry Creek neighborhood. "B2B hardware-as-a-service has trailed behind SaaS, but by taking high up-front capital expenditures off our clients' balance sheets, we can help it catch up."

Baseline purchases the hardware components of an integrated (i.e., hardware, software, and services) technology solution from the seller. End customers can then subscribe to the hardware for much lower up-front cost than buying it outright would be. This also makes the purchase an operating expense, rather than an operating *and* capital expense, smoothing out budgeting and helping increase portfolios' valuations.

Hardware necessarily has a higher cost structure than digital bits, but companies are starting to crack that code.

SUBSCRIPTION RISKS

A subscription model can have substantial benefits for revenue, but it has its risks too. A subscription model only works if expected future revenue materializes.

Salesforce learned that the hard way during the dotcom crash, when a large amount of customers trimmed back spending, canceled their subscriptions, or collapsed.

"Suddenly everything around us was falling apart," says co-founder Parker Harris.[20] Recurring revenue had dried up. Companies that are banking on smaller repeat payments rather than a larger upfront payment for their products and services are especially vulnerable to such an unexpected event.

Success also depends on moving from a transactional customer relationship to a recurring one. Such a shift takes a lot of work and is not without risk. Digitization and revolutions in both channel and data (discussed in later dedicated sections) have made the information inputs required for subscriptions easier to find, but it still requires real work.

Customer lifetime value (CLV) and other such measurements are essential tools for designing a profitable subscription structure. "Customer success" has developed as a business methodology to ensure that customers are achieving their business goals with a given service (and therefore remain sources of recurring revenue).

Ensuring customer loyalty is not an easy task, but it is especially essential for a successful subscription model.

METERED MODELS

Metered pricing, also called usage pricing, pay-per-use pricing, and flexible consumption, is the model of charging and

---

20   Powell 2015

paying based on actual usage of a good. Instead of buying a drill for $90 or renting it for $10 for a day, a customer would be charged for the time the drill was actually used.

While metered pricing has traditionally been common in telecommunications and utilities, increased digitization is allowing many new industries to implement such pricing strategies.

In the software realm, Amazon Web Services (AWS) has a metered pricing component:

AWS offers you a pay-as-you-go approach for pricing for over 120 cloud services. With AWS you pay only for the individual services you need, for as long as you use them, and without requiring long-term contracts or complex licensing. AWS pricing is similar to how you pay for utilities like water and electricity. You only pay for the services you consume, and once you stop using them, there are no additional costs or termination fees.[21]

Notice the messaging around simplicity and ease of use. The goal is to make customers more comfortable with such pricing. Comparing their pricing model to well-known services like utilities increases customers' understanding as well.

---

21 "Pricing" 2019

Metered pricing is entering an increasing number of physical industries as well.

Rolls-Royce, the automotive and aerospace company, was a pioneer of such pricing with its "Power-by-the-Hour" program introduced all the way back in 1962 to support its Viper jet engine. "A complete engine and accessory replacement service was offered on a fixed-cost-per-flying-hour basis. This aligned the interests of the manufacturer and operator, who only paid for engines that performed well," the company explains.[22]

The amount of features and data available today dwarfs that available 50 years ago, of course. By 2016, Bombardier advertised a turbo fan engine equipped with 5,000 sensors generating up to 10 GB of data per second.[23] The abilities of propulsion system manufacturers to monitor how their products are being used and charge accordingly is improving by orders of magnitude.

GE Aviation has its own system called OnPoint, designed to optimize performance and service, that charges by the hour for each engine. Data collected not only helps GE support the engine, but also feeds back into its pricing (this is a relationship we will explore in more detail in the Data revolution).

---

22 "Rolls-Royce Celebrates 50Th Anniversary Of Power-By-The-Hour" 2012

23 Rapolu 2016

"The hourly rate for each engine is based on the time and cycles at enrollment as well as the utilization and flight leg of each operator," according to GE's website. "Hourly rates will vary based on the engine's current time and cycles, time/cycles since last shop visit, operating parameters, operational base and scope of coverage."[24]

Thinking back to Zipcar at the opening of this book, we see that they use a combination of subscription and metered pricing. Membership is a flat amount per month or year, then accessing a vehicle is an additional fee-per-hour of use. Such an arrangement is also referred to as a two-part tariff (entrance fee and per unit charge).

The metric by which metered pricing is charged is an important decision. Potential metrics include per user, per square foot, and per contract, for just a few examples in addition to those used by GE.

It is critical that the metric is aligned with the value provided. For instance, if your company's service promises to increase efficiency but is sold per user, success would actually mean fewer users and *lower* sales. It should go without saying that having a pricing model that fights against your service's goal is the wrong model.

* * *

---

24 "On Point Biz Jets - Details" 2019

Both subscription and metered pricing increase the connection between price extracted by the seller and value created for the buyer. Rather than making a big purchase with uncertainty around its value, a buyer can pay less and risk less. The seller, on the other hand, can appeal to a wider customer base and repeatedly earn for value delivered rather than trying to capture all future value in a single point of time sale.

Increasingly, digitally enabled B2B companies can even offer "success as a service," tying their revenue model to guaranteed customer outcomes. Such approaches de-couple the technology from the customer goal, for instance guaranteeing a certain level of fuel efficiency rather than the method of achieving it.[25]

The Digital Revolution didn't create subscription or metered models, but it has allowed many more companies and industries to adopt them. Digital companies in particular are seeing the writing on the wall, moving quickly from single-purchase to recurring pricing models.

KEY TAKEAWAYS

- Subscription and metered pricing are increasingly pertinent strategies across industries.

---

25 Govindarajan and Immelt 2019

- Both lower the barriers to entry for customers while smoothing out revenue and, when done well, increasing revenue for suppliers.
- Such strategies require a strong commitment to the customer relationship and delivering value.

KEY QUESTIONS

- Could your company attract more and better customers by moving away from single purchase and to a subscription or metered strategy?
- What quantifiable services is your company currently offering that could be monetized through either method?
- How would your company continuously demonstrate the value it is providing customers in such a new pricing system?

Part III

TRANSPARENCY

Chapter 10

DISAGGREGATING TRANSPARENCY

"[C]ompanies need to be aware that jumping on a fad without considering the research is a recipe for failure."

—BEN WABER, PRESIDENT AND CEO OF ANALYTICS
SOFTWARE COMPANY HUMANYZE[1]

In 2016, I received an email from an Irish entrepreneur who had read a piece I wrote about price and pricing transparency.[2] This entrepreneur had started a marketing consultancy and launched a corporate movement calling for "radical transparency" in business, and he wanted to connect about the topic.

I was curious about what he had in mind. While I said our company wasn't looking to join any movements at the moment, I agreed to an email interview that he could publish on his company blog.

---

1   Waber 2018
2   Westra 2016b

When I received his questions, it was clear we were on different wavelengths. His questions presumed that transparency was intrinsically valuable in a business context and that more of it was always better for the customer. If he had understood the article in which I first explored these ideas, he would have known that the issue of transparency isn't that simple.

I responded to his questions with some initial ideas, ones that would later inform this book section. I knew my answers probably weren't exactly what he had in mind, but I thought some nuance and critical thinking would add useful color to his mission.

After all, his website claimed that it would provide "the best transparent content, hand-picked by our team and delivered to your inbox." Despite the early participation in his movement of some marquee names like Zappos, Basecamp, and Patagonia, I was afraid that the entrepreneur wasn't thinking through his concepts clearly enough and would run into trouble.

The interview was never published, and the site went dead later that year.

* * *

Transparency is a perennial topic of admiration among forward-thinking business leaders. The Digital Revolution makes it increasingly important to make proactive decisions when it comes to transparency.

Unfortunately, most discussion around its application in the business world boils down to little more than platitudes:

- *Forbes* says, "[Y]ou should try to disclose everything you can about your prices" in a piece entitled "Transparency In Business: 5 Ways to Build Trust."[3]
- *Entrepreneur* declares: "All businesses that want to build and/or retain the trust of their customers should be working to improve transparency."[4]
- Business executive and author John Gerzema states: "Transparency, honesty, kindness, good stewardship, even humor, work in businesses at all times."[5]

These sentiments sound nice, but they are at best incomplete and largely unhelpful, and at worst incorrect.

The internet has empowered the customer to comparison shop like never before. Price tracking services have proliferated: Camelcamelcamel helps users find the right time to buy a product on Amazon, and Paribus (acquired by Capital One in 2016)[6] enables customers to get refunds on existing purchases when the price drops afterward.

---

3 Kappel 2019
4 Alton 2017
5 Gerzema 2010
6 Perez 2016

Increasingly, industry-level transparency is a given, and businesses must be prepared to defend their pricing based on the value delivered. But as we'll see, more transparency is neither always worse for the company nor better for the customer. Conversely, less transparency sometimes actually improves the customer experience.

Contrary to conventional wisdom, increased transparency in an industry is sometimes self-serving for that industry, too. When prices are public, companies know that undercutting each other on price will likely lead to a price war. Industry-wide transparency therefore can push up prices rather than drive them down.[7]

In this section, we'll add clarity to the role of transparency in pricing and business at large. It is critical to dig deeper into what transparency is and what it isn't. Only then can business leaders make informed choices about what approach is right for their company.

DISAGGREGATING TRANSPARENCY

Transparency is a hot topic, but it's important to disaggregate different meanings of the word in order to have clear conversations and make strategic corporate decisions.

Within the realm of pricing, I want to separate *price* transparency from *pricing* transparency. Many

---

7   "Hospital Prices Are Now Public" 2019

commentators muddle the concepts, but that obscures important distinctions between the two:

- **Price transparency**: when a customer knows *what* they will pay at the onset of the transaction with a given company
- **Pricing transparency**: when a customer knows *how* a given company arrives at a price for a given offering

Most consumer-facing companies strive for *price* transparency. Understandably, consumers want to know how much a good or service will cost before they make a purchase. At the grocery store or the mall, prices are stated ahead of time.

Many meter-based purchases, however, can't have a known price at the beginning of the transaction. They can, however, have a transparent pricing process. For instance, you may not know what your electric utility bill will be at the end of a given month, but you know how the company arrives at that price. This is *pricing transparency*.

It's important to separate the two as well because companies can exhibit one or the other, or both, or neither. Companies can change their approach over time as well.

PRICE TRANSPARENCY

Recall, price transparency refers to having clarity over the price of an offering. Most consumer goods in the modern economy have price transparency. A price tag tells the customer what the price will be at the register.

For a digital example, Amazon makes its marketplace prices very straightforward. Especially for its Prime customers, the price that you see is what you pay, without even a pesky extra few dollars for shipping added during checkout.

Amazon's pricing process, however, is not transparent. We don't know how it decides the specific amount to charge for a specific good. I don't know, for instance, how Amazon and Nespresso together or separately decide to offer an entry-level espresso maker for $119.99. The same goes for most sellers of goods and services. We don't have transparency into their pricing process.

PRICING TRANSPARENCY

Pricing transparency, the visibility of the process that leads to a final price, is more present in metered or usage-based schemes.

Let's take another look at the sister service of Amazon retail, Amazon Web Services (AWS). AWS offers cloud computing services as a platform, essentially allowing other companies to run their IT infrastructure on Amazon's servers. As discussed in Subscription and Metered

Pricing, AWS uses a metered pricing model to offer over 50 digital services, all with their own pricing.[8]

While an AWS customer may not know the amount they will be paying ahead of time, AWS's pricing is transparent down to the hour with detailed pricing tiers and calculators to estimate the customer's monthly bill.[9] Customers may not know the final price until the invoice arrives, but they know exactly how AWS will arrive at that number.

BOTH

Some companies do both price transparency and pricing transparency, showing their customers not only the final price but also how they arrive at it.

As a simple product example, a bundled offer may have a total price as well as break out the regular price for each individual unit. This is some small degree of transparency into how the bundle was priced.

Some companies, such as Buffer, a social media content management service, take pricing transparency even further by laying out exactly how they spend their company revenue and therefore justify their prices.[10] Not only do they publish the monthly price of a given service plan, but

---

8   "What Is AWS" 2019
9   "Amazon EC2 Pricing" 2019
10 Gascoigne 2019

an interested customer could learn a good deal about how they arrived at that number.

Buffer founder Joel Gascoigne was inspired to create a company with a high level of transparency after a bad experience working for an organization that unexpectedly went bankrupt and left its employees blindsided. But even with this inspiration, it wasn't immediately clear what the right level of transparency would be, Gascoigne says.[11]

In 2013, Buffer decided to articulate its values. "And when we did that, we knew that transparency would be a value," says Gascoigne. "[B]ut we decided to phrase it as 'default to transparency,' which is this idea that: Let's flip it around and say everything is transparent unless there's a really good reason why it shouldn't be."[12]

Oliver Cabell, a premium footwear and accessories company, also decided to be transparent in both price and pricing. Its founder, Scott Gabrielson, was moved by the 2013 Rana Plaza factory in Bangladesh that collapsed, killing over a thousand people.

"It gave me the first glimpse into the reality of the fashion industry," said Gabrielson.[13]

"If you're buying from high-end brands at expensive prices, you automatically assume that it's of high quality. It's usually not. And that's crazy," he says. "Transparency

---

11 Allen 2018
12 Ibid.
13 Segran 2016

eliminates any misconception and second guessing, and keeps brands honest."[14]

On its website, Oliver Cabell displays not only the selling price of its products but the company's own costs of production. Shoppers can see exactly how much of their money becomes Oliver Cabell's profit margin. This is also the situation with clothing company Everlane, whose tagline is "radical transparency."[15]

Both brands can attract a certain following with such actions. "There's this lay intuition that when customers find out that a company is making a profit off of them, they might get upset," says Harvard Business School Professor Leslie K. John. "But that's not necessarily the case."[16]

NEITHER

Just as a company may have price transparency, pricing transparency, or both, it of course could have none of the above.

With U.S. consumer health care, most of the time the price of a service is unknown until long after the service is completed and a bill arrives in the mail. Asking a doctor what the price of a given procedure is will earn only a blank stare. This is a lack of price transparency.

---

14 Fraser 2016
15 O'Toole 2016
16 "The Benefits Of Cost Transparency" 2014

The final bill from the insurance company will usually indicate how its total relates to the billed amount and the amount paid for by insurance, but there is very little transparency into how either of those final two were determined.

I experienced this personally with what should have been a simple physical covered by my medical insurance as preventative care. Instead, I received a bill for $900, of which my insurance covered $600. It took numerous phone calls with both the doctor's office and my insurance company even to begin to get a sense of where those numbers came from. (My ordeal was included in a *New York Times* piece on the lack of transparency surrounding medical fees.)[17]

Services that require diagnostics also typically suffer from a lack of both forms of transparency as a fundamental nature of the work. When my car started making a concerning squeaking sound going around turns, I took it to a well-reviewed local mechanic to take a look. I didn't know ahead of time what the bill would be (neither could the mechanic, of course) or how it would be calculated.

CHANGING TRANSPARENCY

Companies can change their approach over time as well. Some companies that have started out exhibiting one type of transparency shift to another.

---

17   Rosenthal 2014

For much of its existence, Uber would not give a rider the final price until after the trip was completed. They would, however, indicate whether any amount of surge pricing was under effect by displaying a multiplier to the normal base rate. Much of Uber's struggle with getting customers to accept this type of dynamic pricing revolved around making them acknowledge the additional price multiplier ahead of time and their acceptance of an unknown final price. This was transparency in pricing only.

Such communication focused the customer on price rather than benefits, which I thought was a losing strategy. I argued in January 2016 that the company should put effort into explaining the benefits of its dynamic pricing.[18] Instead, Uber ultimately decided to hide the dynamic pricing mechanism completely.

As of spring 2016, Uber started to roll out a significant change in its pricing visualization. Currently when customers request a ride, they are shown a single, final price for their trip. No range and no multipliers, only a written notice indicating that prices may be higher than usual when demand is high.

"No math, no surprises," Uber puts it.[19]

So, Uber ditched pricing transparency for price transparency.

---

18 Westra 2016a
19 "Upfront Fares: No Math, No Surprises" 2016

* * *

Putting it all together, we get a picture like this:

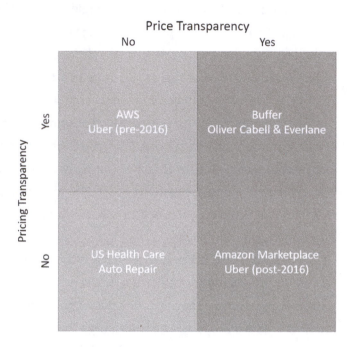

Price Transparency

	No	Yes
Yes (Pricing Transparency)	AWS Uber (pre-2016)	Buffer Oliver Cabell & Everlane
No	US Health Care Auto Repair	Amazon Marketplace Uber (post-2016)

Uber very well could have joined Buffer, Oliver Cabell, and Everlane in the upper right quadrant by keeping the multiplier information *and* presenting a final price. But it didn't.

Is the Uber rider better off knowing the final price without the surge pricing mechanism than having a fuller picture of how the system arrived at the price to quote?

What is the tradeoff between price transparency and pricing transparency? Does increasing one tend to decrease the other?

There aren't any easy answers to these questions, but they're important to consider. We will dig deeper into the ride-hailing case in the next chapter.

Of course, both price and pricing transparency exist on a spectrum. When you shop on Amazon, you see the sticker price and any applicable sales tax and shipping charges. You may not know how those prices are arrived at, but you know how much your credit card will be charged for the transaction. That is clearly more transparent in pricing than the auto repair example, without being close to the transparency of Buffer, Oliver Cabell, or Everlane.

Some industries lend themselves to different levels of transparency as well. When I took my car to the repair shop, the mechanic couldn't have quoted me a price without investigating what the issue was first and what would be required to fix it. Given the solution, I could be given a quote with labor and parts, but there is no clear way to price that accurately beforehand.

With U.S. health care, even if you know what procedure you are having, it is extremely difficult to know what the end price will be. It depends on the provider, methodologies used, and any additional consultations, all before the individual insurance companies and your particular plan enter the picture. It almost certainly doesn't have to be that way, as health care consumers of most other countries already know. But for now, the industry is what the industry is.

TRADE-OFFS

Which type of transparency is better for customers? The answer isn't straightforward.

For each individual transaction, I may find it easiest to have total price transparency: Uber now gives me the total amount I will be charged before I request a ride. Barring a change in destination, this will be the same number that appears on my credit card. That is very straightforward compared to having to think about a potential range of prices or calculating a percentage increase from a base fare.

However, there is a downside for the customer to losing pricing transparency. Without knowing how a surge in demand is affecting your ride, it's harder to compare prices. For instance, if you are going to a new area after work and you see it will cost you $16.51 to leave now, how does that compare to the price of that route at a different time of day? Seeing the price in terms of, say, 1.5 times normal rates gave useful information that is no longer available.

Uber has clearly decided the clarity of a single price trumps knowing how the service arrives at a price. But drivers still see more information about where and when surge pricing is in effect.[20] While it is better for Uber to have customers see one price and not the calculations that go behind that pricing, the same is not true for its drivers. We certainly haven't seen the final iteration of their pricing structure, and it has probably been adjusted since this book was published.

What we can say, however, is that it is insufficient to laud "transparency." We need to clarify what type we're talking about. We also need to investigate whether that transparency is supporting the company and adding to customer value, which we will do in the next chapter.

KEY TAKEAWAYS

- Price transparency and pricing transparency are separate concepts that require separate consideration.
- How a company approaches price and pricing transparency is a strategic decision, not a moral imperative.
- More transparency is not necessarily better for the customer or worse for the company and industry.

KEY QUESTIONS

- Where in the transparency matrix does your company fall?
- Does your company make proactive price and pricing transparency decisions or rely on others' standards?

---

20 Griswold 2016

- How could your company use transparency to create a win-win for itself and its customers?

Chapter 11

TRANSPARENCY AS A TOOL

"Branding is deliberate differentiation."

—DEBBIE MILLMAN, AUTHOR AND DESIGN STRATEGIST[1]

"In ride-hailing, transparency on the customer side is in fact more elusive than one would think," says Stella Penso.

She would know. As the former senior director of revenue and margin management at Careem, the leading ride-hailing app in the greater Middle East and North Africa, Penso was on the front lines of decisions about transparency. She reached out to share her story with me in late 2018 after reading the same article that inspired the Irish entrepreneur.[2]

Her take on transparency was much more illuminating than his, however.

The digital economy has greatly increased the ability of customers to comparison shop. It has also made it much easier for a company to give and change a price quote

---

1   Stein 2017
2   Westra 2016

based on different circumstances, as we saw in the Monetization revolution.

The tendency is toward greater visibility and transparency, but companies still have strategic decisions to make. The core question to answer is, "What level of transparency works for my customers and my business?"

* * *

Penso's experience in the ride-hailing industry shows that more transparency isn't always better, even for customers. To understand this, we first need to see how transparency plays out under both normal and surge pricing.

NORMAL PRICING

For normal, i.e., non-surge, situations, Penso described how ride-hailing apps have essentially two options of how to show pricing. The app could show either:

- An estimated fare range based on predicted traffic and route, or
- A specific upfront fare

The estimate may differ from the final fare. Even the upfront fare, however, may change if the driver substantially deviates from the recommended route or the passenger adds new directions.

Either way, there is a real possibility that the end fare won't be quite what was quoted in the beginning, and neither the driver nor the rider may know ahead of time if that may happen for a given trip.

Any provided estimate anchors the customer's price expectation. Even when the price updates due to a customer's requested route changes, the customer tends to blame the company for unfairly adjusting the price.

"A company may have all the intention to be price transparent, but the actual outcome is up for grabs," said Penso. Providing an inaccurate price in the name of transparency actually harms the customer.

SURGE PRICING

Under surge conditions (when the base fare is increased by a modifier or "peak factor" based on increased demand), transparency becomes even more complicated. According to Penso, there are at least four different ways to display this surge information:

1. The peak factor is completely invisible and simply baked into upfront pricing.
2. The peak factor calculation is invisible, but the app alerts the customer that surge pricing may be in effect.
3. The peak factor is visible as a multiplier (e.g., "x1.1", "x2") that the customer accepts upfront.

4. The peak factor is visible as above, plus the system prompts for an additional acceptance of the peak factor from the customer before final booking.

In terms of pricing, these move from least transparent to most transparent. Careem, perhaps following the conventional wisdom of transparency, originally operated under the most transparent method, Option 4.

They assumed that customers would be more willing to shop with greater transparency provided. In fact, Careem discovered the opposite.

"What we found out during our very transparent phase was that putting the peak factor so much in front of the customer's eyes and making it top of mind was reducing customer's willingness to accept the ride. We were basically scaring the customer off," Penso said.

* * *

What Careem had created for itself was a situation in which transparency was in fact *hurting* the customer experience.

Under normal pricing, the company was providing a fare that it couldn't always keep. Under surge pricing, it was beating the customer over the head.

"While transparency is a good thing, too much of a good thing (even if it is transparency) is a bad thing," Penso concluded. She knew that something had to change.

"We decided to tone down the transparency a bit," she explained. Careem adjusted how it displayed its surge pricing from Option 4 to Option 3. Customers are still alerted about surge pricing, but it is done in a way that doesn't add unnecessary friction to the transaction. Careem saw quick improvements.

"We are now discussing whether we should reduce the transparency a notch more," she said. At the time we spoke and as of publishing, Uber was employing Option 2, alerting the user to surge conditions but not making the calculation visible.

"At the end of the day, the upfront fare estimate doesn't change whether it's displayed as 22 euros or 20 euros with x1.1 peak factor. Why hurt conversion by showing the factor?"

Uber decided to acquire Careem for $3.1 billion in April 2019, shortly before Uber's IPO and pending regulatory approval. This valuation represented an increase in Careem's value of over $2 billion since 2016.[3] Both companies will and should continue to experiment with the right level of transparency to make happy customers and profitable businesses.

---

3   Martin, Nair and Al Ali 2019

"Better customer conversion is good for the whole marketplace as the more bookings a marketplace gets, the more drivers it attracts," explained Penso. "The more drivers, the fewer situations in which surge pricing is needed. Transparency actually affects how appealing a marketplace becomes."

* * *

Transparency is conventionally portrayed as a morality play in which more is always better. It is often construed as benefiting customers at the expense of selfish companies. At times, it is argued that transparency actually helps both customers and companies.

But what the Careem example demonstrates cuts against this conventional wisdom that more transparency is always better. More transparency isn't even always better for customers!

Too much price transparency was harming the market. Both Careem's customers and the company itself are better off with a little more opacity in the process. Over-communication can unnecessarily turn customers off of a transaction that otherwise was at an acceptable price. Amazon, for instance, would only lose sales by having customers click multiple times that they agree on the final price.

The level of transparency should serve the goal of creating satisfied customers; transparency isn't an end goal in and of itself.

TRANSPARENCY AS COMPETITIVE DIFFERENTIATION

Transparency is a hot topic in more industries than just ride hailing, of course.

In a *Harvard Business Review* piece entitled "It's Time to Ban Hidden Fees," author Rafi Mohammed depicts transparency as a moral good that nonetheless hinders companies that adopt it.[4]

"Trying to do the right thing – being transparent and better serving customers – puts a company at a competitive disadvantage. Loading all of the mandatory fees into an advertised price makes it look expensive relative to competitors that opt to sock it to customers later in the purchasing process," he claims.[5]

However, this claim is incomplete at best. In the digital economy where providing transparency is easier than ever, some companies decide that increasing their transparency can be a *competitive advantage*. And serving customers better than the competition is in fact the *only* way to win.

It is up to individual companies to determine what makes the most sense for their strategy and their customers.

---

4 Mohammed 2019
5 Ibid.

For instance, Southwest Airlines has made transparency a core part of its branding. Since 2015, Southwest Airlines has promoted the concept of "trans**fare**ncy."[6] This branding effort even has its own website: www.transfarency.com. I see their large, colorful, cheerful advertisements every time I approach the security line at Denver International Airport.

Southwest proclaims "We're all about being open and honest with Customers and making sure pesky fees stay away from our low fares."[7]

This is a branding initiative centered completely on transparency, both in price and pricing.

6   Jean 2015
7   "Transfarency - Southwest Airlines" 2019

Southwest	Spirit Airlines®
$0 to check one bag	$30 to check one bag
$0 to check another bag (Yep, still free)	$40 to check another bag
$0 for change fees	$110 to change a flight
+ $0 for respect and smiles and maybe a joke or two	$2 extra per bag in summer
	$10 for Spirit to print a boarding pass
	$1–50 to pick a seat
	$1–15 for snacks and drinks
	+ $100 carryon fee at gate
$0*	$294+*
Our low fares actually stay low.	We lost track.

8

Southwest contrasts itself from other airlines that have hidden fees that inflate the final price of a flight. Its goal is to get customers to focus on the simplicity and straight-forwardness of shopping with Southwest.

Note that the airline is not making a claim about its final price being lower than the competition (although it is cleverly implied). The entire marketing push is about being "open and honest," thus making the shopping experience straightforward.

Being easy to transact with is a good characteristic for a business to have. Pavan Arora, at the time the head of content for IBM Watson, put it to me this way: "The more complex you make pricing, the more likely it is that buyers won't spend the time to learn your pricing."

There is a tradeoff in transparency that is similar to that of variable pricing, as we saw in that dedicated chapter.

---

8   Ibid.

There is an opportunity to increase transaction revenue with more complicated or obscure pricing, but the risk is in turning off customers if such pricing appears obscure or nefarious. Consequently, there is a market opportunity for brands that emphasize simplicity.

The airline industry is notoriously low margin, and company profits are highly dependent on the costs of inputs such as jet fuel and labor. While Southwest is known as low-price, it may not always be the lowest for a given leg. Its emphasis on transparency over lowest price is a strategic differentiation that asks customers to focus on competitors' pricing and feel more comfortable with Southwest's, regardless of whether the end result is always that Southwest is least expensive.

Why doesn't every company take Southwest's approach and ditch fees? Well, fees can be very profitable. They can actually better align the value provided to a customer with the price extracted: perhaps someone who checks two bags *should* pay for that additional weight.

This brings us back to the important point that such decisions are dependent on the individual company, its strategic direction, and the relationship it wants to have with customers.

TRANSPARENCY AS MARKET-MAKING

Recall that one of the jobs of intermediaries is bringing trust to the marketplace. If transparency increases trust, then there is an opportunity for intermediaries to provide value to marketplaces by providing transparency.

Cars.com and similar services make it easier for customers to compare the prices of different vehicles and the overall offerings of different dealerships. By making it easier for customers to comparison shop, such services increase the transparency in the market.

"The Market for 'Lemons,'" a seminal economics paper from 1970 by UC Berkeley Professor George Akerlof, describes the messiness of the used car market.[9] Due to information asymmetry, customers had high uncertainty of the quality of car they hoped to purchase. Dealers had trouble demonstrating and proving quality, so they couldn't charge higher prices for such quality. This decreased the incentive to provide quality vehicles in the first place.

The upshot was that both car quality and customer willingness to pay suffered, causing the entire market to decrease in value. Customers shopped as if every car were a lemon; dealers had no way to demonstrate value and were forced to compete on price rather than quality.

Improving transparency would help to solve this problem by increasing dealer credibility and more clearly connecting value and price. This would help dealers command higher prices for quality cars while helping customers avoid lemons. Akerlof predicted in the paper that "private

---

9   Akerlof 1970

institutions may arise to take advantage of the potential increases in welfare which can accrue to all parties."[10]

When Mitch Golub, founder of Cars.com, started out, he wasn't sure how car dealers would react. Conventional wisdom was that sellers hated transparency. Golub was pleasantly surprised, however, at the reaction he received.

"The curious thing about the dealership partners was while some were mad about some of the transparency we provided to consumers, the vast majority of dealers were very happy to see us come on the scene," Golub explained to me. "There were a lot of players in the marketplace that weren't on the up and up, and transparency hurts those players the most."

Greater transparency in the used car marketplace helped to punish unscrupulous dealers. Well-performing dealerships could increase their performance and differentiate themselves more clearly from the rest. By making it harder for low-performing dealerships to persist, greater transparency helps to increase the quality and reputation of the entire industry.

Akerlof won the Nobel Prize in Economics in 2001 for his research on asymmetrical information began with "The Market for 'Lemons.'" The success of Cars.com and other services in increasing the quality of the used car

---

10 Ibid.

market through transparency further demonstrates Akerlof's thesis.

Years later, Akerlof would describe the value of such transparency-increasing services thusly: "[W]hen we can measure the qualities of the goods, services, and assets we buy—or when those qualities can be accurately graded, and we also understand those qualities and grades—then, for the most part, we get what we expect."[11]

Bringing greater transparency to industries can be an opportunity for intermediaries to add value to both sides of the marketplace.

TRANSPARENCY AS OPPORTUNITY

While the digital economy has made price and pricing more visible than ever, transparency is still a tool. If we acknowledge that such transparency is a tool, it follows that it must be managed strategically.

Companies must understand that it is increasingly hard to hide pricing and price points. Fewer customers than ever want to jump through hoops to understand a company's pricing. Even in B2B and complex sales, there is less appetite for opacity and hiding pricing behind a lead request or lengthy negotiation.

Even many car dealerships, once the epitome of price negotiation, are moving toward straightforward "no haggle"

---

11 Akerlof and Shiller 2015, 137

pricing. Such dealers may not always be the least expensive, but many customers hate the negotiation so much that the simplicity and transparency in "no haggle" pricing is worth paying a little more.[12]

For dealers, some of this is accepting that with price transparency online, they cannot afford to juggle multiple prices and accurately segment customers on the fly. On the plus side, if simpler prices also increase the speed of selling, then sales reps have more time for the next sale, meaning more revenue for the dealership.

Many businesses fear transparency. Others embrace it as a competitive advantage. Still others base their entire business models around providing transparency to an industry. Transparency isn't inherently good or bad, but decisions made about it are strategic differentiators.

If your company has low price and/or pricing transparency, that isn't necessarily bad. Perhaps it is a function of industry necessities or how the service is delivered (recall the health care and auto repair examples from earlier).

Many companies simply never communicate their prices, preferring to bury it in layers of negotiation or reveal it only after a lengthy quoting process. This lack of transparency turns away many potential customers, however.

---

12   McParland 2017

Alternatively, if your company would like to be easy for customers to buy from, increasing its transparency may be an opportunity to do so while differentiating itself from the competition.

* * *

Just as price is an important aspect of branding and marketing, so is the amount of transparency of both price and pricing. Different industries lend themselves to different levels of each, but especially with consumer markets there is a strong push toward price transparency.

Radical transparency is not a moral imperative, but increasing transparency may be a business opportunity. Companies can earn more and better customers when they make buying straightforward and honest. Intermediaries can add value to entire marketplaces by increasing the ability of buyers and sellers to trust and transact.

The Digital Revolution is increasingly making transparency the default, and it is incumbent upon you to meet that challenge head-on.

KEY TAKEAWAYS

- Price and pricing transparency is a tool, not a moral imperative.
- The level of transparency a company presents must be a strategic decision and be reevaluated over time.

- Transparency should serve the customer and can be a strong competitive differentiator for companies that treat it strategically.

KEY QUESTIONS

- When was the last time your company reevaluated its degree of price and pricing transparency?
- Is there an area in which too much transparency is actually hurting the customer experience?
- How is your company differentiated from the competition based on transparency? How should it be?

Chapter 12

HIGHLIGHTING VALUE

"[D]etermine what your customers need and work backward, even if it requires learning new skills."

—JEFF BEZOS, FOUNDER AND CEO OF AMAZON[1]

As we learned in the previous chapter, companies need to make decisions about how to make price and pricing transparency work for themselves and their customers. Contrary to what you may hear from business luminaries, there is no simple moral imperative to adopt higher price or pricing transparency in a given company. There is no one-size-fits-all.

Transparency as a whole is certainly increasing across industries, however. So, what does apply to every company is the realization that this increased transparency accentuates the importance of value in pricing.

In increasingly transparent industries, companies need to have done their homework to defend their pricing decisions and demonstrate the value that they provide. This

---

1   Salter 2009

involves switching mentalities from *cost-plus pricing* to *value-based pricing*.

Let's explore the difference and why value-based pricing is requisite in the digital economy.

COST-PLUS PRICING

Many industries have operated or continue to operate under some concept of cost-plus pricing. This refers to pricing that starts with the cost of the product or service in mind and adds on some acceptable margin.

First, the company develops a new product that it believes its customers will want. From the production process, the company determines the fixed and variable costs of producing the product. The required margin is set by expectations of return on investment or industry standards. A price that will bring in that margin is determined. Then the commercial team goes out to find a customer who is interested.

This is a simplified version of how many companies still operate. Yet it is not inaccurate. I have seen it in action, to the detriment of the companies in question. It is also very common in government contracting.[2]

One of the major disadvantages to this approach is that both the price and the customer are something of an afterthought, with the product in development regardless. The value to the customer better be above the resulting price, otherwise there will be no market for the product to begin with!

Cost-plus especially makes no sense when the variable cost of producing the good is near zero, such as with software and pharmaceuticals. Yes, both industries can require heavy R&D expenditures, but customers are not responsible for your company's cost structure. And the marginal cost of a software install package or a pill is vanishingly small.

Anyone who has ever bought software or medicine knows that the price can be anything but. That's because they are priced not on cost, but on value.

VALUE-BASED PRICING

Value-based pricing takes the process of cost-plus and flips it around. With value-based pricing, you start at the value to the customer and work backwards.

---

2   Kendall 2018

First, a relevant customer is identified and their needs understood. A price the customer would be willing to pay for a solution to their needs is determined. Margin expectations are set, and that is used to calculate what the cost of supplying the product would have to be. Then, the company can create a suitable product that fits the requirements.

Marketing luminary Seth Godin sums up this approach as: "Don't find customers for your products, find products for your customers."[3]

Again, this is a simplified but not inaccurate illustration of how customer-centric and value-based companies approach their market and their product development.

One of the major advantages of this mindset is that by the time a company has invested in a product, it already has identified relevant potential customers and an appropriate price based on their willingness to pay. The risk of finding oneself with a product that either doesn't have a market or can't be sold profitably is much smaller.

Of course, the ceiling of potential price is much higher when taking a value-based perspective for the same reasons that cost-plus makes particularly no sense for low marginal cost industries. Enterprise software and

---

3   Nelson 2016

breakthrough pharmaceuticals can find strong demand in the market despite prices in the tens of thousands of dollars because they focus on the value delivered, not the cost to produce.

Value-based pricing is clearly superior to cost-plus pricing in the vast majority of situations, but many companies and industries are stuck in the old mindset. Indeed, many companies who say they operate under value-based pricing have adopted the right language but not the right practices.

Much of the consulting work I do depends on establishing a foundation of value-based pricing. Without such a foundation, a company is helpless against disruption.

Details about the analytical tools used for value-based pricing are beyond the scope of this book, but one of the best is called Economic Value to Customer (EVC). This is a method of determining (and, crucially, quantifying) the differential benefits between a new offering and the next best alternative. Not only does it enable executives to better understand the offering from customers' perspectives, but it also is a powerful tool for salespeople to have a value-based discussion with prospective buyers.

Conjoint analysis is a survey-based statistical marketing methodology to quantify the value of different product attributes. Importantly, it does so without directly asking respondents direct questions about their willingness to pay (as is the case with tools such as Van Westendorp and Gabor-Granger). Answers to such direct questions suffer from well-known biases and lack the precision of a proper statistical technique.

At the end of the day, value-based pricing depends on accurately understanding what value customers consider.

BEHAVIORAL PRICING

Behavioral economics has become an especially prominent topic in popular science due to its marriage of traditional economics with counterintuitive insights from psychology. The application of such insights to pricing is called *behavioral pricing*. (This is not to be confused with behavioral-based segmentation discussed in Chapter 6: Variable Pricing.)

One well-known example is the center stage effect, which states that customers will tend to choose a middle option when presented with three or more options. The middle option appears as a reasonable compromise between the smallest (or cheapest) option and the largest (or most expensive) option. This effect can be seen in everything from menu ordering to product versioning.

Another example would be anchoring. Anchoring occurs when an individual is influenced by an initial number on later decisions. For instance, shoppers may purchase more of an item when it is marked "limit of ten per person" than without such a limitation, because that "ten" serves to normalize purchasing that many of the item. Another example would be a store in which every item is always on sale that still includes a list price on the tag. A $25 item looks like a better deal when we are told it is normally $35. The $35 anchors shoppers at a higher price.

In a 2018 marketing stunt, Payless ShoeSource, a discount footwear retailer, convinced a group of customers to spend hundreds of dollars on their products by rebranding themselves as a luxury Italian brand named "Palessi."[4]

"I would pay $400, $500. People are going to be like, 'Where did you get those? Those are amazing,'" said one woman surveying a pair of shoes that normally retail for $30.[5]

It was an amusing and light-hearted prank, but also illustrates how malleable customers' perceptions can be according to circumstance and how companies can manipulate that. The stunt unfortunately didn't stop Payless from declaring bankruptcy in early 2019.[6]

Behavioral pricing, at the end of the day, is taking advantage of psychological and perceptual peculiarities of being human to influence purchasing behavior. How should we think about this in terms of transparency and value-based pricing?

While behavioral methodologies are not secret, companies typically don't broadcast their usage, so I would consider behavioral pricing not aligned with transparency.

4   Phillips 2018
5   Ibid.
6   Hirsch 2019

That isn't to say it is bad, just that a strategy that depends on behavioral pricing techniques doesn't lend itself to pricing transparency. If your company is aiming to increase its pricing transparency, it should rely less on behavioral pricing approaches.

An important additional point: behavioral pricing techniques are tactics, not strategy.

Deciding how to present different versions of a product is an important decision, but first comes the hard work of determining what customers value and how to solve their problems in a profitable manner. It is easy to be distracted by clever applications of behavioral pricing and forget the core issues of how to delight customers. The risk of such an approach is having a well-designed menu selling products no customer wants, or clever marketing stunts that add nothing to the bottom line.

"Consumers are more empowered and informed than ever before, and any pricing strategy that seeks to fool or mislead them is unlikely to be successful for long," says Greg Loewen, CEO of pricing software company Digonex.[7]

If you are looking for a hack to get around customer value, you won't find one.

---

7   Walker 2017

IS THERE ANY ROLE FOR COST?

Even under a value-based pricing framework, there can still be a role for cost in pricing decision making.

As a baseline, cost becomes a go/no-go hurdle for pursuing an initiative. If the value to customers is less than the cost to produce, generally speaking, that is not a product to pursue. Working from a value-based pricing framework for product development enables companies to abandon an initiative if it doesn't look profitable *before* the product is realized.

There are some situations in which there is a compelling cost-based story that can be used to justify a price change to customers. Such a story can only be part of the overall value message, of course, and must be reasonable. One situation is when costs for an entire industry increase. This can become the basis for price increases even though the value to the customer hasn't changed.

If there is a sudden frost in Florida, the price of orange juice may increase. Customers can understand more expensive oranges mean more expensive inputs to orange juice and that they see higher prices as a result. Airlines and logistics companies will sometimes have fuel surcharges to account for fluctuating costs of fuel that affect their entire industries.

There is a *price elasticity* point to be made here as well, referring to how strongly customer demand reacts to change in price. Price elasticity at the product category level is lower than the price elasticity at the brand level. For example, customers will switch between brands of toilet paper for relatively small price differences, but it takes a much larger price increase across all brands to go without toilet paper at all. If the price of paper pulp increased across the board, the paper products industry as a whole could increase price without much change in customer demand.

Another situation is when the cost to serve varies by customer. A business customer who purchases in small amounts from a manufacturer may have higher unit prices than a bulk buyer. Even with the same volume, it costs more to send multiple small shipments than one large one. Smaller orders are costly to the manufacturer, so it is reasonable that at least some portion may factor into the price offered to customers who order in that manner. This is related to behavioral segmentation we saw in Chapter 6: Variable Pricing.

Cost can also be part of the story told to a customer to explain price changes. Researchers have found that "consumers do believe that prices are based on costs," even if theory and practice says costs should have little or no role.[8] Speaking to this belief, especially in cases like those described above, can be effective.

---

8   Obermiller, Arnesen and Cohen 2012

This cost belief can cut against a company's aims, though. In October 2018, Tesla made the Performance Upgrades Package for its Model 3 car free. That package previously sold for $5,000.[9] The Performance Upgrades Package includes some different hardware from the base model, but a significant portion of what you get is simply a software update unlocking new performance.

Many customers who had paid $5,000 for the upgrade clearly thought that price was justified by the extra cost to Tesla, because many were upset by the sudden drop in price. Such swings in price without a change in the corresponding product can be disorienting for new customers and aggravating for existing customers who paid full price.

"It definitely shakes my trust in Tesla," stated one customer.[10] Another customer succinctly complained: "[U]p and down pricing is annoying."[11]

For some customers, such moves cut against Tesla's branding: "It seems like half of them don't see a problem and the other half agree that it goes against Tesla's claim of a clear price structure to differentiate themselves from the dealership model," writes Eletrek's Fred Lambert.[12]

Generally speaking, price should be about value. Value-based pricing enables the supplier to earn better

9 Lambert 2018
10 Lee 2019
11 "Model 3 Performance "Upgrade Package" Is Now Free." 2018
12 Lambert 2019

margins and it properly reflects value to the customer. But cost can still have a role to play, so long as there is a reasonable story behind it.

* * *

Technology and digitization are massively increasing the imperative for value-based pricing. For digital companies, that is because cost-plus pricing is nonsensical in a world of low marginal costs. For traditional companies, technology is forcing their hands due to competition and customer demands.

In order to sell based on value, a company must understand the value of its products. Product management, marketing, and sales teams must be rowing in the same direction under shared understandings of product value in order to drive profitability.

Remember, value is always from the customer's perspective. If you don't understand your customers, you will fail to meet their needs.

Clear communication tends to go both ways. If you want your customers to believe in your value, it must be demonstrated. Obscuring prices and pricing makes it more difficult for customers to understand your value story, but communicating them in a confusing way can unnecessarily turn off customers as well.

KEY TAKEAWAYS

- Increased price and pricing transparency at the industry level highlights the importance of value-based pricing.
- Value-based pricing is an essential strategy to serving customers profitably, especially with increased digitization.
- Cost, when communicated well, can support a pricing story, but at the end of the day your customers are not responsible for your cost structure.

KEY QUESTIONS

- Is your company operating under a value-based pricing mindset? If not, how can you get it there?
- If your company's pricing is overly dependent on behavioral pricing tactics, how can you elevate this to the realm of strategy?
- If your industry suffers a cost shock, do you have the processes and mechanisms in place to adjust your prices accordingly?

Part IV

CHANNEL

Chapter 13

CHANNEL PARTNERS

"The job of the channel(s) is to find, win, make, keep and grow happy customers."

—HANS PETER BECH, AUTHOR AND BUSINESSMAN[1]

"He needs to stop and take a breath. If you're an internet billionaire, maybe you think the world revolves around you, and the world springs from your laptop."[2]

Jim Appleton, president of the New Jersey Coalition of Automobile Retailers, was upset. In March 2014, Appleton was waging war against Tesla and its CEO Elon Musk, who wanted to sell his vehicles directly in the state and not through franchised dealerships as required by law.

"Well, I got news for him. This is not a new law, Tesla is operating illegally, and as of April 1st, they will be out of business unless they decide to open a franchise," Appleton declared.[3]

---

1   Bech 2015, 22
2   Popper 2014
3   Ibid.

By April of that year, sure enough, Tesla was banned from selling its vehicles directly in New Jersey.[4] It looked like Appleton had won.

"Mr. Musk is a brilliant man, and Tesla is an innovative company. We can all respect that," Appleton said. "But he doesn't get what it takes to do business in New Jersey. With all due respect, his legal opinions are about as sound as my programming abilities."[5]

Less than a year later, however, New Jersey reversed course and allowed Tesla to open direct sale dealerships.[6] As of February 2019, Tesla has delivered just under 10,000 vehicles to customers in New Jersey.[7] The company, although subject to divergent analyst opinions, is not out of business in New Jersey or elsewhere.

Dealers are singing a different song than in 2014. In California, dealership group Sonic Automotive president Jeff Dyke summed up the 2019 state of dealers' new opinions on Tesla during a disappointing earnings call: "My hat off to them -- they're selling a lot of cars, and there is no question in California that it's getting in our shorts."[8]

* * *

---

4   Welch 2014
5   Popper 2014
6   Popper 2015
7   Khemlani 2019
8   Coppola 2019

Distribution channels are chains of businesses that get products or services from the supplier to the end consumer. The companies that act within these channels are called *channel partners.*

Channel partners are a type of intermediary that assist with one or many of the commercial operations of a supplier. They facilitate marketing, selling, distributing, and servicing the supplier's products. Distributors, wholesalers, and retailers are all common examples of channel partners.

In short, channel partners help a company reach and serve its end users.

Many industries have had more or less set channel relationships, due to certain dynamics of the market (e.g., grocery stores acting as retailers for food producers), legal requirements (e.g., the three-tier alcohol distribution system in the U.S. mandating separation of production, distribution, and retail), or a mixture of both (e.g., car dealerships in the U.S. being required retailers but also a system that has made sense for serving disperse geographies and distributing expensive, hard-to-ship vehicles).

In the digital economy, such historical assumptions no longer hold. Traditional channel relationships are being disrupted. What was unthinkable only a short number of years ago is becoming reality.

In the story above, Tesla decided that the dealership distribution model is no longer relevant and doesn't fit its company strategy. It has succeeded in breaking industry expectations and consequently creating a competitive advantage.

Before we examine that case and others more closely, however, it is important to understand more thoroughly the purposes of channel partners.

PURPOSES OF CHANNEL PARTNERS

What is the benefit of having channel partners?

The core tasks of customer engagement can be broken into five categories:

- **Inform**: The market must be aware that an offering exists. Branding, advertising, and communication are all key tasks under inform.
- **Interact**: Someone must physically or digitally interact with your customers. That includes explaining the value proposition, developing sales materials, and engaging the customer, for example.
- **Transact**: Getting the deal done. This may include price negotiation, completing a contract, and processing payment information.
- **Deliver**: The process of getting the product from the supplier to the customer. Especially for physical goods, someone must hold inventory in advance, breaking bulk amounts into the proper transaction size, and handle the actual logistics behind final delivery.
- **Service**: This includes all support that occurs after the completion of a given order. Customer service and

technical support are both aspects of this category, as are customer success and account management.

These five functions are all essential tasks for a commercial organization. They may be done by the supplier or by a third party channel partner, but they must be performed by someone. If the supplier doesn't do one of these tasks, a channel partner must. Conversely, if a channel partner doesn't, the supplier must.

Who should do what? That comes down to who can do each function most efficiently. If a channel partner can provide a service more efficiently than your organization, it is a better use of resources for it to do so. A startup selling an advanced new product may find it useful to outsource many of its channel functions, such as payment processing and logistics. However, it may choose to keep customer service in-house if the company is uniquely positioned to help customers with its own product.

These relationships can reasonably change over time, too. Our hypothetical startup in the previous paragraph may be especially dependent on channel partners early on to focus on product development, but bring them in-house as the company matures and develops different areas of expertise.

REWARDING CHANNEL PARTNERS

Channel partners, of course, must be compensated for the value they provide. Each of the five channel functions comes at a cost. Critically, the reward channel partners receive should be commensurate with the value provided. That may seem obvious, but I regularly come across companies who cannot articulate why exactly they are ceding large amounts of margin to channel partners.

Not infrequently, when I ask clients what tasks their distributors are performing, what value they're adding to the market, I'm met with blank stares. I get variations of "We *have* to use them," "That's just how the industry works," and "We've always used those groups."

I also hear from companies trying to find ways to change their distribution relationships. "We want to be closer to the end user," they say. Sometimes, the very companies that bemoan the end user distance think their company is stuck in inherited channel relationships.

But that assumption should be challenged, as Tesla has done in its industry. Just as good channel partners can make your job easier, bad ones can make it much harder.

If distributors are adding little value while capturing a large percentage of product margin, your company may be able to do better without them. If channel partners are not providing value, your company should look for ways to remove them from your commercial operations.

Channel strategy needs to be clearly defined. Where are your company's comparative advantages? What is your company, frankly, lousy at providing?

This is the consideration that Tesla and many other companies are making: whether to blaze a different trail. They are deciding to eschew the traditional channel relationships in their industries because they no longer add sufficient value in the digital economy.

KEY TAKEAWAYS

- Channel partners assist a supplier in marketing, sales, distribution, and service to a final customer, as well as cross selling opportunities.
- Channel partners should be compensated according to the value they provide in the five key channel functions.
- Digitization and technology are opening up new channel possibilities for companies to implement, circumventing unhelpful channel partners.

KEY QUESTIONS

- Can you articulate the value that your channel partners are providing your company, or are they "just how the industry works"?
- Are there channel functions currently being done by your company that could be better handled by a channel partner (or vice versa)?

- If you could redesign your company's channel structure from scratch, what would it look like?

Chapter 14

CHANNEL AS A CHOICE

"It's OK to have your eggs in one basket as long as you control what happens to that basket."

—ELON MUSK, CEO OF TESLA AND SPACEX[1]

It is incumbent on companies to put real strategy into how they manage channel relationships. Following the status quo is insufficient.

Channel partners must be adding value. There are too many opportunities for differentiation to accept that "the way it's been done" in your industry is therefore the way your company has to operate.

The relationship between companies and the customers, as well as how they serve those customers, has dramatically increased in complexity thanks to the Digital Revolution. Concurrently, some companies are finding that bucking the traditions and trends in their industries can create windfalls. There are more options than ever to shift

---

1   Chafkin 2007

functions, tasks, and subtasks to channel partners, or have the supplier absorb more of these roles itself.

TESLA'S CHANNEL UPRISING

"This Musk guy, he wants all the profits for himself," said Tom Dougherty, a dealership salesman, during Tesla's clashes with New Jersey law described in the last chapter. "They wanted to go direct, which means no sales force. That's cutting out a lot of people."[2]

Removing dealerships from the car selling experience does in fact cut out a lot of people. And Musk surely does want to increase the share of profits that go to Tesla. His strategy, hearkening back to the Reintermediation revolution, is in fact to "cut out the middleman."

Tesla is revolutionary not only for being the first all-electric car company, having the first U.S. automotive IPO since Ford's in 1956, and creating fantastic vehicles, but also for overturning the traditional manufacturer-dealership distribution model.[3]

"For all the talk of Tesla's product innovations, it is leading another battle: this one centered on how vehicles are sold, as much as how they're made," writes *Fast Company*.[4] This assault on the dealership channel model is as transformative for the industry as the push for electric vehicles.

---

2   Popper 2014
3   "Tesla Becomes First U.S. Auto IPO Since Ford" 2010
4   McCorvey 2016

Starting from scratch gave Tesla the opportunity to assess aspects of the automotive industry that were taken for granted or seen as impossible to change. Tesla looked at the dealership model and decided it could perform those channel partner functions better on its own.

One stumbling block has already been mentioned: by law, car manufacturers must sell through dealerships. This is only one of many legal protections given to dealerships by every state in the U.S. While the details may vary from state to state, the bottom line is manufacturers cannot sell directly to customers. Channel partners are mandatory. This means that Tesla has also had to fight in the courtroom and in the field of public perception rather than simply on business merits.[5]

Tesla is a company of the digital age and therefore thinks in terms of digital-first. So, it takes a unique approach to the functions traditionally done by dealerships. Let's look at how Tesla handles each of the five channel functions:

INFORM

Tesla utilizes online presence, word of mouth, heavy press coverage, and showrooms in major cities to inform customers about its value proposition. By creating the "iPhone of the electric-car market," Tesla draws potential customers

---

5   Ellig and Martinez 2015

in via branding, other happy customers, and the intrigue of seeing its products on the streets, not by dealership marketing and promotion.[6]

An electric car is most useful in heavily populated areas that can provide the charging infrastructure needed to keep the car moving. Dealerships every twenty miles make the most sense to cover wide and hard to reach geographies, which Tesla has already decided aren't in its target market.

For customer education, traditional dealerships built around the sale and service of gas engine cars probably aren't the most natural evangelists for electric vehicles.

"We actually train people to educate," Musk says about his employees. "It takes them at least twice as much effort to sell someone an electric car and to educate them as to why an electric car is good. And so if we were to go through the traditional dealer path, the result would be a disaster."[7]

INTERACT

Tesla is largely comfortable utilizing digital resources for customer interaction. Its product innovation draws the type of customer they want to attract in the first place. Tesla is an elite brand, so it counts on customers self-selecting for those who are willing to come to it on its own terms. Most interaction is done through Tesla's own website.

6   Ferris 2019
7   "Why Texas Bans The Sale Of Tesla Cars" 2013

In major cities, again, there are showrooms to view and test drive cars, because there is no substitution for in-person when it comes to a large purchase like a vehicle. Whereas traditional dealerships tend to be on the outskirts of urban areas and consist of large car lots, Tesla showrooms are centrally located and utilize a small store footprint, saving on cost and contributing to the urban and elite brand perception.

"Because Tesla sells its vehicles directly to customers instead of using independent dealerships, the company has more control over its stores and the way they present the brand to consumers than other automakers do," according to *Business Insider*.[8] This control is a major benefit for a high-value-brand company such as Tesla, as similarly positioned Apple has found with its product development and storefronts.

TRANSACT

In many states, Tesla is not allowed to sell its cars from its showrooms. Interested customers can only purchase their car through Tesla's website. Such laws are changing, though, as we've learned, and Tesla takes an active part in pushing for those changes.

Tesla recognizes that in today's economy, customers are more and more comfortable making such large purchases

---

8   Matousek 2019

online. "Ordering your Tesla is just like any buying experience on the Internet," Tesla's website explains.[9] In a world where 99% of automotive shoppers expect their purchase process to be a "hassle," Tesla makes buying a new car as simple as we would expect from a digital-first company.[10]

"When the customer is ready to purchase, they do so on their in-store digital design center and a salesperson can walk them through the entire process," explains customer insights company Qualtrics. "The customer can also purchase the vehicle from Tesla's website in the comfort of their own home, and the prices are non-negotiable."[11] (Recall from Chapter 6: Variable Pricing how fixed prices can be a differentiator for elite brands.)

Some states do allow Tesla to sell a limited number of vehicles directly, and more are reevaluating their existing laws, so expect to see some change here in the next few years.[12] Tesla is also playing around with the idea of only selling its cars online and doing away with store sales completely, which the company says would enable it to lower prices by 6%.[13]

Regardless, Tesla will continue to own its own shopping experience, whether online or through its own showrooms,

9   "How Ordering Works" 2019
10   Jeffs 2015
11   Kaemingk 2018
12   Lambert 2018
13   O'Kane 2019

delivering a better and more streamlined shopping experience than a channel partner could provide.

DELIVER

One of the big benefits of a dealership is the car you purchase is sitting right there. In most cases, when you buy a Tesla, you're not going to see the car soon, let alone drive it off the lot.

"[Showrooms]... carry a small number of cars in inventory for customers who wish to drive away with a Tesla immediately," according to the company.[14]

For everyone else, the process is much what one would expect buying any other product online. "When your car is ready, it will either be shipped to your home or to the nearest Tesla service center," Tesla states.[15]

This is a very big break from how people are used to buying vehicles, but not a change from how many people order most other items. It also saves on a dealership function: the cost of holding inventory (which may or may not sell).

Tesla doesn't need big dealership lots to distribute its vehicles, which is yet another strike against the relevancy of such a channel arrangement for the company.

---

14 Lunden 2019
15 "How Ordering Works" 2019

SERVICE

One of the major channel functions dealerships play is in servicing vehicles. If your Ford or Toyota has an issue, odds are that wherever you live in the U.S., there is a Ford or Toyota dealership nearby that can help.

If your Tesla needs a repair, where do you go? An average mechanic isn't going to have the familiarity, let alone the extra parts, to service the car adequately.

Tesla does have service centers, but in large swaths of the country, you may have a long drive to find a repair:

16

---

16 "Find Us" 2018

As of November 2018, there are 79 Tesla service centers in the U.S.[17] By comparison, Ford has over 3,000.[18]

While Tesla plans to open more as it moves into more mass-market vehicles, it would have a long way to go to reach that kind of footprint. But does it need that kind of coverage?

For typical dealerships, much of their profits come from the service and financing departments, not actual car sales.[19] Tesla rejects this approach. "I have made it a principle within Tesla that we should never attempt to make servicing a profit center. It does not seem right to me that companies try to make a profit off customers when their product breaks," Musk wrote.[20]

And as already stated, Tesla focuses its customer acquisition on urban areas with higher population density. Customers who live far from a service center can still order a car, but they are not the primary target customer.

So, if Tesla's service strategy doesn't require thousands of dealerships, why pay for them?

* * *

17   "US Tesla Service Centers" 2018
18   DeBord 2017
19   "Where Does The Car Dealer Make Money?" 2019
20   Musk 2014

In total, we can see how Tesla decided its channel goals wouldn't be served by a dealership model. Instead of taking the industry's organization around dealerships as table stakes, it figured out how to cut dealers out completely and save the channel margin for itself.

Other car companies, despite fighting such changes, may be realizing that such a strategy could work for themselves as well. Morgan Stanley analyst Adam Jonas says that "most auto companies would love to sell vehicles the way Tesla does. There's just one catch. They can't. It's against the law."[21]

Consequently, Tesla leading the charge against dealership laws may have the effect of reshaping channel dynamics for the entire industry.

KEEPING FOOD OUT OF GROCERY STORES

Tesla is a prominent example of a company redefining channel expectations, but such cases are not confined to large consumer purchases such as a car. The same changes can be seen with the food we eat.

"Wow, wow, no cow," sings Oatly CEO Toni Petersson, sitting at a keyboard, surrounded by fields of grain, in a 15-second promotional video with over 2.3 million views.[22]

Oatly is a brand of oat milk from Sweden. You may be thinking oats don't produce milk, but neither do almonds

---

21   Sheetz 2019
22   "Toni TV - Wow No Cow" 2017

or soybeans. Similarly, oat milk is used as a milk substitute, especially in higher end coffee.

Growing revenue from $1.5 million in 2017 to over $15 million in 2018, with a further doubling expected in 2019, Oatly is demonstrating how to use the power of the digital economy to find its customers without first depending on traditional channel partners.[23]

Let's look at how it approached its entrance into the U.S. market in 2016.

INFORM

Oatly's inform strategy was to use high-end coffee shops as channel partners, rather than trying to reach coffee drinkers through retail such as grocery stores, where you would typically find dairy and dairy substitute products. Oatly's non-traditional product and exclusive brand benefited from hip baristas being the cutting-edge expert who could recommend Oatly to their customers.

Their product is instantly noticeable with big playful lettering on the carton. "We didn't have a large budget, and we had to use the package as the main medium," creative director John Schoolcraft says. "They were basically in-store billboards."[24]

Oatly has also experimented with urban advertising, such as building murals and wheat paste posters, which

23 Weissman 2019
24 Entis 2018

pokes fun at the brand itself and is memorable to viewers. By appearing in uncommon environments and not depending on typical advertising for food, Oatly can further differentiate its brand and control its messaging.

INTERACT

Originally, high-end coffee shops were the only place where customers could interact with the brand. Customers couldn't walk into a grocery store and find Oatly on the shelf.

It may seem like the right kind of traditional channel partner, such as Whole Foods, could have been workable for Oatly. But the grocery world is so competitive, it can easily take more than a year of toil just to appear on a shelf.[25] Staying on that shelf is even harder. What kind of support your brand will get is dependent on how much you are willing to pay. Oatly decided it wasn't worth the expense.

As Vice puts it, "The move proved ingenious, as baristas became ambassadors of the oat milk gospel without feeling like sales representatives to customers."[26] Oatly created greater demand via this method than it could hope to reach in a mass market grocery aisle setting.

---

25 Thomson 2017
26 Orlow 2018

TRANSACT

The grocery business is notoriously cutthroat and low margin. Avoiding that channel and selling through coffee shops and its own website kept Oatly's costs down and its premium brand perception up.

Going to Oatly's website directs the user to "Oatfinder," a map and search page for finding nearby coffee shops serving the oat milk. "[W]e made this map in order to help you to find all the forward thinking coffee shops around the world that are currently serving Oatly," the page states.[27] The list of premium café channel partners helps to associate their brands with the Oatly brand, reinforcing both's sense of exclusivity.

Purchasing Oatly felt special, exactly because it wasn't available in traditional channels.

DELIVER

Delivery depended largely on the inventory held by coffee shops. Due to the time involved in making the product and the surge in demand, Oatly routinely was unavailable.

These shortages only served to strengthen the special and unusual nature of the brand and the product. A twelve-pack of Barista Edition went for $226 via a third party on Amazon during one shortage.[28]

---

27 "Oatfinder" 2019
28 Settembre and Wolfson 2018

Oatly may not have intentionally contributed to these supply issues, but certainly benefited branding-wise from their effects.

SERVICE

Oat milk doesn't require service contracts and maintenance, but like any product, someone needs to provide customer service. Oatly handles that itself in its typical quirky and low-key manner.

For a time, the carton print included the personal email address of creative director John Schoolcraft.[29] Customers could reach out directly with their questions, comments, and complaints. Such an atypical closeness with the consumer emphasizes that Oatly cares about its customers.

* * *

Forgoing traditional channel distribution didn't stop Oatly from a quick expansion. The *New York Times* reported in January 2018 that "Oatly has spread from 10 locations in New York to more than 1,000 locations nationwide," less than a year after it landed in the U.S.[30]

Having 1,000 locations pales in comparison to Oatly's footprint if it had teamed up with grocery retail, but, like Tesla, Oatly didn't need to be everywhere to serve its

29 Entis 2018
30 Wertheim 2018

chosen customers. Oatly could simply achieve its goals more efficiently on its own and via select coffee shops.

As of 2018, Oatly is beginning to be available in traditional retail, and it may be only a matter of time before it is available at major coffee shop chains. But by entering the U.S. with a specific channel strategy that eschewed these partners, Oatly was able to establish its presence, develop its brand power, and be in a much better position to negotiate with channel partners down the road.

KEY TAKEAWAYS

- The Digital Revolution ensures that companies have more options than ever for reaching their customers.
- Companies such as Tesla and Oatly are able to control their brand, win customers, and earn more margin by approaching their channel relationships strategically.
- No industry's channel partnerships are set in stone. They must be evaluated for the value provided.

KEY QUESTIONS

- What industry changes are threatening the way your company interacts with its customers?
- How do you manage your relationships with your channel partners?
- If you are a channel partner, how can you demonstrate the value you are providing to your suppliers?

Chapter 15

THE ELEPHANTS IN THE ROOM

"It is rare to find a business partner who is selfless."

—*MICHAEL EISNER, FORMER CHAIRMAN AND
CEO OF THE WALT DISNEY COMPANY*[1]

Having value-creating channel partners is much better than the alternative. But even good partnerships carry risk. In the channel, one of those risks is that the partner becomes more powerful than the supplier.

"Booksellers initially thought of Amazon as their best friend," writes author Franklin Foer. "They were coming in and they were challenging Barnes and Noble, and Borders, which were the big, dominant corporations of the day... but they could never envision that Amazon would overtake them all."[2]

There are two immediate dangers of having too powerful a channel partner:

1. That the partner becomes so dominant it can appear indispensable

---

1   Orlic 2016
2   Lane 2017

2. That the partner becomes the gatekeeper between your company and your customers

Let's look at each of these in greater detail.

WHO HAS THE CHANNEL POWER?

One of the keys to success for Walmart a generation ago and Amazon now is their seeming indispensability. Over 90% of Americans live within 10 miles of a Walmart.[3] And 56% of shoppers in the United States first visit Amazon when shopping for an item.[4]

That incredible presence gives both companies unparalleled customer exposure. Suppliers feel Amazon and/or Walmart must be their channel partners, which puts suppliers in a weak negotiating position. Customers may love Amazon, but many sellers feel like they simply don't have a choice: Amazon's just the place to be.

When a distributor has inordinate power in so many channel roles, it makes it harder for the supplier to maintain their own brand, customer relationships, and pricing strategy.

It is estimated that Amazon lost $2 *billion* on its customer-facing retail marketplace in the first quarter of 2018. As one stock analyst opinion piece put it, "Amazon clearly doesn't care about making money from its retail

---

3   Ladd 2018
4   "Amazon's Ambitious Drive Into Digital-Advertising" 2018

business."[5] What does that mean for everyone else in Amazon's ecosystem?

Perfect Price's Alex Shartsis describes Amazon as having a "winner-take-all pricing strategy." That affects pricing strategy at all retail businesses that compete with Amazon, which is, essentially, all retail. Most retail operations don't have a sister company like strongly profitable Amazon Web Services to offset their losses, however.

So, if you are hoping to maintain good margins on the products you sell through Amazon or another massive distributor, you are fighting an uphill battle. What are your options?

One key approach is to focus on brand power.

Oatly, the oat milk company from the previous chapter, provides one example of a company working hard to establish its brand *before* transacting with traditional channel partners. Warby Parker is another.

Warby Parker, maker of fashionable prescription glasses, worked hard to develop its brand. (It is also a fantastic example of reintermediation in the vein of Dollar Shave Club.) Part and parcel with its branding has been the decision *not* to sell through retailers such as Amazon and Walmart.

At first, Warby Parker only sold through its website. More recently, the company has experimented with its own

---

5   Kee Jr. 2018

brick-and-mortar stores, which is still an unusual step for an online company to take when most physical retail stores are suffering. Wouldn't opening a physical store hurt its online sales, too?

"Once we open a store, we see a short-term slowdown in our e-commerce business in that market," according to Dave Gilboa, co-founder and co-CEO of Warby Parker. "But after nine or 12 months, we see e-commerce sales accelerate and grow faster than they had been before the store opened. We've seen that pattern in virtually every market."[6]

By having a physical presence, they are doing something that (so far) Amazon cannot do: interact experientially with customers.

(Amazon, of course, is experimenting with its own brick-and-mortar stores. The giants are not complacent.)

Both Oatly and Warby Parker focused on their brands and customer experience so that they would have more power in their relationships with channel partners. They want customers to seek out their brands, not happen upon them via a powerful channel partner like Amazon.

WHO OWNS THE CUSTOMER RELATIONSHIP?

Regardless of your channel strategy, it is essential that your company stays close to its customers, no matter what.

---

6   Foster 2017

There is no faster way to lose relevance than to lose track of what your customers truly value.

If your channel partners are too dominant, they can control the access your company has to its own end users. Losing these relationships can be disastrous.

"Not being in tune with your customers is like living in an alternate reality," according to author and businessman Bo Bennett. "[T]he way you think your customers feel about your product is not always the same as what your customers really think about your product."[7]

If your channel partners end up doing all of the customer-facing work for you, then your customers really belong to them. The channel partners will be the ones who most intimately understand the changing needs, concerns, and priorities of your customers. Your ability to stay on target will be weakened.

Turning to the software world, MuleSoft, provider of integration enterprise software, is largely dependent on implementation channel partners such as Deloitte, Accenture, and Capgemini for actual delivery and service. As these partners spend a good deal of time with the actual customer, they can have an outsized influence on customers' decision making. This puts MuleSoft in a precarious position.

---

7   Bennett 2018

On the consumer software side, music streaming company Spotify has filed a complaint against Apple for how it operates its App Store platform. Spotify claims that Apple coerces apps to use its expensive payments system by imposing technical restrictions on apps that don't, and therefore favors its own service, Apple Music.[8] Since Spotify must use Apple as a channel partner to reach iOS users, its channel power is weakened.

Recalling the Dollar Shave Club example from Chapter 9: Subscription and Metered Pricing, channel relationships present an issue for traditional razor manufacturers, too. "The incumbents are kind of trapped," says venture capitalist David Pakman. "Gillette really can't sell directly to customers because they can't tick off the retailers."[9]

The power of retailers was and continues to be a concern for Oatly, which leads the company to interact heavily and directly with its customer base via social media. Such interactions can help not only with branding but also with customer feedback.

"[B]y connecting with our consumers on social media, we get closer to them and are able to involve them on a whole other level," says Sara Hansson, the global social media manager at Oatly. "This allows us to build a

---

8   Ek 2019
9   Isaac 2014

long-term bond with our customers that are more critical to our future success than you could ever imagine."[10]

Staying close to their customers is a common problem for hospitality and airline companies as well, which get much of their bookings through online travel agency (OTA) channel partners such as Expedia and Orbitz. To complicate matters further, there are also global distribution system (GDS) intermediaries that coordinate transactions between the service providers and OTAs. These layers provide real value, but also complicate the customer relationship.

When a transaction goes through a GDS, the airlines "don't get a lot of information about that customer," Jackie Storm, the team lead for domestic pricing at American Airlines, told me. "The system and technology are not there yet."

The GDS layer is old, but entrenched. The airline industry is working with GDS partners on ways to better capture and maintain more customer information, as well as better merchandise products.

Airlines and hotels want to promote their brands and have relationships with their customers that go beyond being the lowest price on Expedia for a given search. Agreements with GDSs called "full content agreements," however, restrict airlines from advertising lower fares on

---

10 Komfo 2018

their websites than appear on channel partner OTAs. This means that price typically cannot be used as an incentive to drive direct purchases. How can you encourage customers to buy direct, then?

Some airlines, such as Southwest, simply doesn't use OTAs. Like Warby Parker, a customer must buy direct from their website. Delta Airlines has pulled its fare and scheduling information from certain OTAs while continuing to partner with others.[11]

Special perks and conditions are also used to encourage direct sales. These, writes journalist and travel expert George Hobica, "include offering more frequent-flier miles or points if booked directly with the airline, promo codes which can only be redeemed on the airlines' websites, and ticket discounts (for example, British Airways offers lower fares to AARP members, but only if booked at BA.com)."[12] In some cases, certain flight legs may only be available to certain credit card holders or airline status holders.

Some hotels too are experimenting with only offering rewards to customers who buy direct through the hotel's own website.[13] This may help customer loyalty, but it puts the supplier in direct competition with its own channel partners. Such an adversarial position may not be sustainable.

---

11   Martin 2015
12   Hobica 2017
13   Jet 2017

Tesla's channel decisions also highlight its customer focus and how that supports its product innovation. "We like the idea of owning the entire process," says Ganesh Srivats, Tesla's vice president of North American sales. "It creates an information loop from our customers straight into manufacturing and vehicle design."[14]

We will learn more about the feedback cycle this creates next in our Data revolution.

KEY TAKEAWAYS

- Dominant channel partners come with their own problems: indispensability and gatekeeping.
- A supplier focusing on its own brand and customer engagement can help to protect its power within the channel.
- Getting regular and actionable customer feedback is essential for product management and development.

KEY QUESTIONS

- Does your company have access to unfiltered customer data, or is it received through an intermediary?
- How easy is your company to communicate with for your customers?

---

14   McCorvey 2016

- Does your company conduct Voice of Customer (VoC) or other customer research to stay on top of what its customers prioritize?

Part V

DATA

Chapter 16

THE NEW OIL

"Data will become the biggest production material in the future, it will become a public resource like water, electricity, and oil."

—JACK MA, CO-FOUNDER AND EXECUTIVE
CHAIR OF THE ALIBABA GROUP[1]

Uber is the world's largest taxi company without owning a single car. Cars.com facilitates thousands of transactions but doesn't own any cars itself. Priceline and Upside connect travelers to hotels and flights without managing any property or airlines.

In an important sense, these companies are not truly in the business of supplying consumers with the goods and services sold on their two-sided platforms. They are in the business of *data.*

Rana Foroohar, global business columnist and an associate editor at the Financial Times, writes:

---

1   "Alibaba's Ma Says Data Resource Is Oil, Water Of The Future" 2015

What is the fastest growing part of the American economy today? The answer is the gathering, analysing and selling of our digital data.

The extraction of Americans' personal data — the most valuable resource in the world today — is worth a whopping $76bn in yearly revenue [...] If the current trends hold, our data will be worth $197.7bn by 2022 — more than the total value of American agricultural output.

That is resource extraction on a massive scale. If data is the new oil, then the US is the Saudi Arabia of the digital era. The leading internet platform companies are the new Aramco or ExxonMobil. Google, Facebook, Microsoft, Amazon, Verizon and Twitter drill for their digital oil by watching everything we do or say on the internet.[2]

Such technology platforms, built for one purpose, can be applied to numerous others. Such data-empowered companies are reintermediating many industries already, as discussed earlier in this book. And in Jeff Bezos's famous formulation, today is still only "Day 1" for Amazon, meaning the company is only just getting started.[3]

Data services are the near future battlefields for the companies that provide them. As *The Economist* writes:

---

2   Foroohar 2019
3   Kline 2017

Information technology comes in cycles, each giving rise to a new computing platform. In the current cycle, the key component—or the next platform—is data. Facebook may have started as a social network, Google as a search engine and Microsoft as a maker of operating systems and other software. But today they all deal in data...the firms are quickly becoming fully fledged data distilleries: they suck up as much digital information as they can, crunch it in vast data centres and turn it into artificial-intelligence services.

[...]

More information lets firms develop better services, which attracts more users, which in turn generate more data. Having a lot of data helps those firms expand into new areas, as Facebook is now trying to do with online dating. Online platforms can use their wealth of data to spot potential rivals early and take pre-emptive action or buy them up.[4]

The delivery company UPS is a less anticipated example of a company that uses reams of data to improve its own service. UPS's delivery trucks are equipped with sensors that document and measure all manner of activities to find opportunities for optimization. Such connectivity is illustrative of the Internet of Things (IoT). It is estimated

---

4   "How Regulators Can Prevent Excessive Concentration Online" 2018

that there will be over 26 billion connected devices by 2020, collecting and analyzing all manner of data.[5]

"The data are about as important as the package for us," says Jack Levis, UPS's director of process management. "Just one minute per driver per day over the course of a year adds up to $14.5 million."[6]

IoT technology will have an enormous impact on B2B and industrial sectors, too. "Not only is more data created by industry than in the consumer world, it's more valuable," argues technology strategist Bhoopathi Rapolu. "[T]he data created by industrial equipment such as jet engines, gas turbines and MRI machines has more potential business value on a size-adjusted basis than other types of big data being generated from the social web, consumer Internet and other sources."[7]

The importance of data can pop up in some surprising places. While most traditional advertising has suffered in the Digital Revolution (recall newspaper classified advertising and Cars.com in Reintermediation), billboards are holding steady. Owners can get critical location data from viewers' smartphones, which is used to inform larger aggregated profiles. Advertisers can better target specific segments or react to external conditions: "Billboards can

---

5   Morgan 2014
6   Goldstein 2014
7   Rapolu 2016

be programmed to show ads for allergy medication when the air is full of pollen," writes *The Economist*.[8]

Data is important for companies of all sizes as well. Both Scott Case's Main Street Genome and Cherian Thomas's Spotluck discussed in the Monetization revolution aim to enable small businesses with the data to make better decisions: the café underpricing its coffee needed data to fix its self-inflicted wound of $25,000.

APP-BASED MOBILITY SERVICES

There is a gold rush for data, and companies that can best generate and use data will have enormous impacts. The incredible growth and valuation of ride-hailing companies is the perfect illustration of this fact.

Uber, Lyft, Careem, and others in the industry are clearly not taxi companies. But they're also not really simply ride-hailing companies. They are more broadly described as "app-based mobility services."[9] Ride-hailing serves as a method for collecting data and building systems to serve value in areas much wider than ride-hailing.

"We see the Uber app as moving from just being about car sharing and car hailing to really helping the consumer get from A to B in the most affordable, most dependable, most convenient way," Uber CEO Dara Khosrowshahi said after the acquisition of e-bike sharing company JUMP,

---

8   "Billboards Are An Old But Booming Ad Medium" 2018
9   Stoll 2019

adding, "[B]ecoming a top urban mobility platform is part of Uber's ultimate vision."[10]

Urban mobility, of course, is much wider than ride-sharing, be it via car or e-bike. Uber Eats, Uber's food ordering and delivery service, has gone from 3% of Uber's revenue in 2016 to 13% two years later.[11] Uber has been able to utilize its ride-sharing platform to innovate in an adjacent but heretofore separate industry. No taxi company ever tried getting into deliveries, after all.

"We can't really be the Amazon for transportation without the biggest mode of transportation out there, which is public transport," argues Uber transit team leader David Reich. "The vision is to be an all-in-one app for all your transportation needs."[12]

"Cars really were, for us, a kind of starting place," according to Uber transportation policy and research chief Andrew Salzberg. "Once we've built this platform for mobility there are a whole host of business lines we can build beyond that."[13]

In addition to "urban mobility platforms," companies such as Uber are also referred to as "transportation network companies" (TNCs), managers of intermediary platforms that connect millions.

---

10   Dickey 2018
11   Webb 2019
12   Chapman 2019
13   Ibid.

"As administrators of these networks, Uber and Lyft have also had access to an incalculable stash of data on the behaviors of riders and drivers, the streets they travel on, the businesses they visit, the products they consume, and everything in between," argues *Forbes*. "Based on the companies' performance so far, it's clear that maintaining this mass flow of data — and removing any legal barriers — is their actual long-term strategy."[14]

This brings us back to the likes of Amazon. "You think Amazon sells stuff. They do not," argues economist Michael C. Munger. "They license software."[15]

It is not hard, therefore, to see how companies such as Amazon and Uber will be increasingly going head to head against each other, as well as against other data platforms. They are all in the business of how best to connect buyers and sellers.

FROM DATA TO INSIGHTS

Companies use data to find insights. For example, UPS uses its data to find insights on operational savings.

Seagate Technology, a data storage company, predicts that the amount of data created *every year* will increase from 33 zettabytes in 2018 to 175 zettabytes by 2025 (one zettabyte is one trillion gigabytes).[16] But as data continues

---

14 Burns 2019
15 Munger 2018, 66
16 "Dataage 2025 - The Digitization Of The World" 2019

its astronomical growth, insights will become harder to come by and consequently only more valuable.

"Data itself is valuable, no question. But it's the insights that matter," Cargill's Lynn Guinn told me. "It's what you learn from it, what you take away from it, what you apply from it, and how you monetize it."

If data is like oil, then insights are like all manner of products made from refining oil. Fertilizers, perfumes, plastics, soaps, asphalts, and synthetic rubbers represent just a handful of product categories derived from petroleum. The consumer usefulness and producer profit margins for such products are much higher than for the raw material. The same goes for data and its dependent products.

"Data experiences the same economic transformation as oil," according to Bill Schmarzo, data expert and CTO at Hitachi Vantara, a data systems company. "Raw data needs to go through a refinement process (cleanse, standardize, normalize, align, transform, engineer, enrich) in order to create "curated" data that dramatically increases the economic value and applicability of the data."[17]

Such refinement takes a lot of work, but it is critical to unlocking the real benefits of data for customers. Such work greatly increases the value on the table.

"To create value from oil, the oil must first be refined," Schmarzo continues, pointing out that high-octane fuel

---

17 Schmarzo 2019

can be almost twenty times more valuable than raw oil. "Oil in and of itself is of little consumer or industrial value," he states. "It's only through the refinement process that we get an asset of value."[18]

According to Schmarzo, providing a customer with raw data is like pumping raw oil into a car. We don't expect cars to refine their own oil. Why expect data customers to handle raw data instead of giving them something directly actionable?[19]

Companies that depend on data need to consider how their business goals could be better met with more refined information. If a company can provide value-added insights rather than raw data, it can create a much more valuable product.

UPSCALING CROWDSOURCING

When Daryn Nakhuda founded Spare5 in 2014, the goal was simply to create a better crowdsourcing platform than the tools that were then available. He had used Amazon's crowdsourcing tool, Mechanical Turk, first at an earlier startup of his and then at Amazon itself when the company acquired his startup.

The promise of crowdsourcing, according to Mechanical Turk (MTurk)'s website, is making it "easier for individuals and businesses to outsource their processes and jobs

18 Ibid.
19 Ibid.

to a distributed workforce who can perform these tasks virtually."[20] The website also notes:

> *This could include anything from conducting simple data validation and research to more subjective tasks like survey participation, content moderation, and more. MTurk enables companies to harness the collective intelligence, skills, and insights from a global workforce to streamline business processes, augment data collection and analysis, and accelerate machine learning development.*[21]

"The concept was always appealing," Nakhuda told me. "But the execution left a lot to be desired. It wasn't easy to use, and the output was low quality."

Spare5 introduced "an app that enables everyday people to perform short tasks on their smartphone — like photo tagging, price guessing, and sentiment analysis of text — in exchange for payment."[22] Spare5 made several key innovations in its platform compared to the other tools available, but perhaps the most important one was focusing on the quality of its output.

"From the start, we thought rather than charging companies for the number of crowdsourced participants, we'd charge for a good answer," Nakhuda said. "Let us figure

---

20 "Amazon Mechanical Turk" 2019
21 Ibid.
22 Soper 2017

out how many people to ask and how to determine quality; the customer shouldn't have to worry about that."

"We pay participants for their contribution, and our customers pay us for a good answer," Nakhuda added. "We're doing value-based pricing." Or, using Schmarzo's analogy, they are not expecting their customers to refine their own oil.

Not all of Spare5's clients found their value-centric approach useful. Some companies just wanted "good enough" and fast answers. The clients that did see the value tended to be working on one particular problem:

"They were all building datasets for training AI," Nakhuda told me. "That's where we decided to shift and focus on that customer segment. Obviously, turnaround time and cost are still important for them, but they understand that building a high quality dataset is critical."

Spare5 became Mighty AI in January 2017 and since has focused on serving customers training AI for autonomous vehicles via over 200,000 users around the world.[23]

Training autonomous vehicles requires very detailed datasets that correctly identify all manner of obstacles and signage. Mighty AI's crowdsourcing enables that. As *Inc. Magazine* describes their work:

---

23   Stewart 2017

Mighty AI is a computer vision company that trains artificial intelligence programs to better see and understand the world. That way, it can better differentiate between, say, a paper bag blowing in the wind and a cat trying to cross the street. The startup pays people to perform simple image recognition tasks on their phones or desktops. For a few cents or dollars per task, a person might receive an image of a city street and be asked to outline all the pedestrians, cars, street signs, or whatever objects the system requests. That info is then used to strengthen data sets for firms developing computer vision technology, including self-driving car companies.[24]

It may be surprising that such work is still done by humans, let alone a decentralized network of amateurs. But currently, humans are still able to discern the relevant information in images much better than an algorithm.

"The holy grail for AI would be unsupervised learning, where the machine absorbs the data and just knows what to do with it," Nakhuda says. "But the technology isn't there yet." Until then, crowdsourced platforms like Mighty AI are essential tools for burgeoning technologies like autonomous vehicles.

"I think our investors are looking at us as providing picks and shovels to the AI goldrush," CEO and co-founder

---

24 Ryan 2018

Matt Bencke explains. "No one knows exactly where the gold is, but everyone knows you need picks and shovels."[25]

"Training data isn't the sexiest part of AI," Bencke admits. "But it is vital." If AI doesn't have good data from which to learn, Bencke concludes that you basically only have a "really expensive data science team."[26] Making sure the data is good and selling their insights according to that value makes Mighty AI an essential partner.

This is one area in which data will continue to be valuable: training AI and machine learning. Like UPS, Amazon puts intense focus on improving the efficiency of its operations. Jeff Bezos reportedly asks every executive yearly to answer the question: "How are you planning to use machine learning?"[27]

But Mighty AI is an illustrative example of a company upscaling from providing simply data to serving actionable insights. Providing insights versus raw data is valuable for customers; consequently, such companies can command higher prices for their services.

The question of how to price such services and data in general will be addressed in our next chapter.

---

25 Soper 2017
26 Ibid.
27 "Amazon's Empire Rests On Its Low-Key Approach To AI" 2019

KEY TAKEAWAYS

- Digital platform companies are truly data companies — their business models and competitive advantages depend on their ability to harness data.
- Data is the raw material for insights, and the differential value between raw data and actionable insights will only grow.
- Companies that are able to sell insights as well as data are well-poised to take advantage of this dynamic.

KEY QUESTIONS

- Recalling the examples of Uber, Amazon, and other two-sided platforms: what business is your company in, really?
- What data sets created by your company could become more valuable internally and externally through curation into insights?
- What decision-making processes does your company have in place to translate data and insights into business judgments?

Chapter 17

MONETIZING DATA SERVICES

"Converting Facebook data into money is harder than it sounds, mostly because the vast bulk of your user data is worthless."

—*ANTONIO GARCIA MARTINEZ, BUSINESS AUTHOR*
AND FORMER FACEBOOK PRODUCT MANAGER[1]

"Information has historically been very difficult to price. From the days of Gutenberg to New York Times Digital, it's been a struggle," said Pavan Arora.

When I spoke with him in 2018, Arora was Chief Data Officer for IBM Watson, IBM's artificial intelligence (AI) program, that burst into public consciousness in 2011 by beating reigning champions in the game show *Jeopardy!*. Arora's job was deceptively simple: figure out how to monetize IBM's data.

"It's always been difficult to price data, and it gets more difficult now as the multiplication of data types increases," he told me. "We're not just talking about a corpus of

---

1   Garcia Martinez 2019

knowledge, we're talking about a raw version, an enriched version, and the insight."

"Data is absolutely exploding, but there is a lack of a data strategy," says David Dittman, director of business intelligence and analytics services for Procter & Gamble. "Getting the right data that you need for your business case, that tends to be the challenge."[2]

The growing importance, accessibility, and value of data leads to the question of how companies can best monetize their data for use by others. As a baseline, Arora told me, companies need to rethink what metrics they use to charge for their services.

TRADITIONAL DATA PRICING

The first step is recognizing what valuable data your company may be generating and putting a price on it. "If digital information lacks a price, valuable data may never be generated," *The Economist* argues.[3]

"Typically, data deals are at present worked out between someone holding the information and those who want to extract insights from it," *The Economist* explains in another piece. "Such deals can be clunky to set up, however. They tend to concentrate on datasets that hold obvious value."[4]

---

2   Schuman 2017
3   "Data Is Giving Rise To A New Economy" 2017
4   "New Ways To Trade Data" 2018

One typical way of pricing access to data or an API has been volume-based, either quantity-based or pay per access instance. Another has been simply licensing access irrespective of actual usage.[5] Recalling the Monetization revolution, however, gives us a glimpse of the inadequacies of such an approach.

Arora presented an example using Bloomberg Professional Service, the financial data source otherwise known as the "Bloomberg terminal."

"Let's say Bloomberg sells via a per-seat volume pricing model. Then, with automation and other changes, a major client drops from 75,000 to 40,000 people," Arora suggested. "Bloomberg has just lost millions on that pricing model for no good reason."

Such a counterproductive pricing model recalls the importance of pricing by the correct metric, as was mentioned in Subscription and Metered Pricing. Pricing by the number of people accessing data is insufficient to capture the value Bloomberg is delivering in this scenario.

At the same time, charging for access to data increasingly doesn't make sense in a world with crushing amounts of data. "Pure information is not going to be valued in the same way as it used to be, because of its proliferation and accessibility. The value will be in the assessment and application of it," Arora argued.

---

5   Kushal, Moorthy and Kumar 2011

At SAP, the multibillion-dollar enterprise software company, I spoke with Kyle Garman about the company's monetization. As their senior vice president of global business development, Garman has seen many changes over a decade with the company. He is also a partner with multiple venture capital and private equity groups, including Andreessen Horowitz and Bain Capital, affording him both a deep and wide view across the software and data pricing landscape.

"I have been very involved in how SAP does and thinks about pricing. It's unbelievably complex," Garman said. "We have over a thousand metrics that we use for pricing different software solutions, let alone services."

As we saw in the Transparency revolution, such complexity can be counterproductive, and that is something SAP is aware of, too. "While we have made great strides in simplifying our pricing models, some have jokingly suggested that you need a PhD to understand how we set up our pricing and contracts," Garman said.

Thinking through better ways of serving and monetizing data and data services is critical, however.

"Traditional data pricing models don't work for data in the current world," Arora admitted. "It's a difficult and confusing time."

VALUE-BASED DATA PRICING

The imperative for value-based pricing exists for data services just as it does for other products, and for the same reasons. Customers don't care about your cost structure. They care about the value that your product or service delivers them.

Garman explained to me how SAP uses many different pricing models to try to get at this value, "everything from licensing, to subscriptions, to outcome-based pricing, and everywhere in between." We already saw in the Monetization revolution how some of these models and many more can be used to drive value.

"We do a lot of value engineering. We tell customers to look over the next few years and see the quantifiable business impacts we bring," Garman said. "We try to make the discussion much more about their profit improvement of $1 billion, for example, that will cost them significantly less. That's how we seek to negotiate: profit or cost takeout, not number of users or revenue."

Garman spoke about one of SAP's largest customers as an example of pricing toward the value of the solution. "All of their technology is wrapped around SAP. So, while they only have however many thousands using an SAP interface, their entire company of hundreds of thousands accesses the data," he told me. "If we had a pricing model that was only based on using an SAP interface, we would not be getting our fair share of the enormous value we're creating."

This contrasts nicely with Arora's Bloomberg example. Volume-based data pricing, as the example shows, is akin to cost-plus pricing. It is only loosely associated with the value delivered. Conversely, determining how the end user is generating value from using your services and claiming your fair share of that value will lead to improved data monetization.

INSIGHT VALUE

The importance of value is even more apparent when we revisit the difference between raw data and an insight.

Harvard Business School Professor Theodore Levitt popularized the adage that customers don't buy a drill because they want quarter-inch bits but because they want quarter-inch *holes*.[6] Insights are the hole; data is the drill.

"If I'm looking for Twitter sentiment on Apple, I really don't want to sift through all of Twitter. I need the insight. I should pay for the insight," Arora said. "At the same time, if I do need access to everything behind the insight, I should pay for that, too. If I access it a million times, I should pay for that. And if I redisplay it or resell it as part of a larger product, I should pay even more."

---

6   Levitt 1969, 1

Arora also used the Dodd-Frank Act, the 2010 U.S. federal law concerning financial regulation, to illustrate the diverging importance of data from insight:

"Dodd-Frank is over 2,000 pages long. People don't want to read it; they want to know what obligation it brings for their businesses," Arora explained to me. "Just because the pages are widely available doesn't make the analysis any less valuable." Data may be easily accessible, in other words, but the insights aren't.

"So how do I price extracting the right obligations from Dodd-Frank and matching them to your business? That's not an easy task," Arora said. Neither is determining the value of the Apple insight via Twitter.

But the insights, as with refined oil products, are much more valuable than the data behind them. Pricing becomes more complex for high-value data, in no small part because the audience for that type of data is so much more specialized. The job of the data or insight provider determining what value customers are deriving from their information becomes much more complicated but only more important.

And customers who see the value in them, like autonomous vehicle companies with Mighty AI, will pay for that value. How customers determine the value or quality of insights isn't easy; unlike gasoline, the quality isn't easy to know beforehand. But with experience comes better understanding.

"Companies will come to IBM Watson, see our services, and say 'no, no, it's too expensive. We'll do it ourselves,'" Arora told me. "And then a couple months later, they're back at our doorstep. 'Yeah, I'll take it,' they say. 'We haven't moved. We haven't gotten anywhere.'"

No user values data for data's sake. The user wants the data to tell them something: they want an insight. Paying for insights is aligning price with what the customer truly values. Such thinking is a natural application of value-based pricing, but applying this to data requires careful consideration.

* * *

Remember: the product offered may not simply be the data services, either. Companies must think broadly about what types of benefits they truly offer and how different customers may value those.

For Mighty AI, that includes the value of their crowdsourcing platform itself.

"Traditionally, a lot of people have thought about us as a data provider and they're paying for the data," Nakhuda explained to me. "We weren't pushing them to think about us as providing insights and an underlying software and analytics platform in addition to the data."

"The tool we built, the user interface, the workflow engine, the templates... all of these are valuable," he continued. "Giving companies access to these materials and letting them have their own setup and community is interesting to many customers. That's a different pricing opportunity to capture different pieces of value than simply data or insights."

The imperative to price data services on value is clear, even in today's world. And it's soon to become stronger than ever as automation and digitization continue to change the nature of businesses.

AI and machine learning depend on an enormous amount of data input. The results can be stunning: in one medical experiment, AI trained on CT scans was 94% accurate in detecting lung cancer, more accurate than the doctors.[7]

"How can you set up your services for a world where the customer might be a machine?" Arora rhetorically asked. Such questions should be on the mind of anyone selling data services.

DANGERS OF DATA

There are, of course, dangers in the external use of data, both in the courts of law and public opinion.

As of publishing, Facebook's Cambridge Analytica scandal (in which the political consulting firm improperly accessed and used the data of 87 million users) is still

---

7   Grady 2019

being investigated for fraud, and new investigations over Facebook's data agreements have begun.[8]

This is not an environment that investors or executives envy. And it's one that rightfully angers millions of users, who feel taken advantage of and violated.

Google is increasingly coming under scrutiny for data practices, too. As the world's largest digital advertising company providing a vast range of enterprise and consumer products, Google collects even more data than Facebook. It can be hard to control what information is shared, let alone disengage completely from its ecosystem.[9]

Even Apple, known for its privacy protections, falls short for many customers. In one exposé, technology columnist Geoffrey A. Fowler found that his iPhone was very actively sharing his information:

> On a recent Monday night, a dozen marketing companies, research firms and other personal data guzzlers got reports from my iPhone. At 11:43 p.m., a company called Amplitude learned my phone number, email and exact location. At 3:58 a.m., another called Appboy got a digital fingerprint of my phone. At 6:25 a.m., a tracker called Demdex received a way to identify my phone and sent back a list of other trackers to pair up with.[10]

---

8   LaForgia, Rosenberg and Dance 2019
9   Kelly 2018
10   Fowler 2019

The external use of data has real risks. Whether to monetize data services must be a careful strategic consideration.

Recall how we saw in Chapter 7: Individualized Pricing that Groupon, despite having the ability to enact such a model, decided it wasn't aligned with the company's customer engagement strategy. Similarly, certain companies with the means to monetize their data nonetheless decide not to do so.

Netflix, for instance, collects reams of consumer data, but uses it only internally to strengthen its very popular recommendation engine, which in turn increases customer engagement.[11] According to *Fortune*:

> *Instead Netflix crunches the consumer data it holds to aid its recommendation engines and to decide what additional programs to commission. Netflix doesn't want to share that data with anyone else. It sells no advertising and releases no ratings. It cares about finding an audience for its show, though. Not for nothing, Netflix is a lavish marketer, spending heavily on advertising across digital, print, and broadcast media.[12]*

Despite its data being very valuable to advertisers, its consumer data is simply not for sale.

---

11 Burgess 2018
12 Pressman and Lashinsky 2018

The same, so far, goes with Amazon, which has helped keep it out of the cross-hairs of regulators and angry customers, at least as far as data practices are concerned. According to *The Economist*:

> *Amazon collects and processes customer data for the sole purpose of improving the experience of its customers. It does not operate in the grey area between satisfying users and customers. The two are often distinct: people get social media or search free of charge because advertisers pay Facebook and Google for access to users. For Amazon, they are mostly one and the same...*[13]

The external use and monetization of data has its dangers. The familiar theme of promise and peril that permeates this book may be the most relevant for the Data revolution.

KEY TAKEAWAYS

- Monetizing data services, as with other products, requires careful consideration of the value provided.
- The value of an insight will only increasingly diverge from the value of raw data, as the latter explodes in volume and complexity.

---

13 "Amazon'S Empire Rests On Its Low-Key Approach To AI" 2019

- To maximize profitability, it is crucial to consider all aspects of value delivered to customers, not just that derived immediately from the data or insight.

KEY QUESTIONS

- What steps is your company taking to determine the end-user value of the data services it provides?
- What customer segmentation exists among your customers in terms of how they use your company's services and derive value from them?
- What enrichment, cleaning, or other value-add can your company provide to its raw data to increase its value to users?

Chapter 18

KNOWING THE CUSTOMER

"[T]here is no guarantee against product obsolescence. If a company's own research does not make it obsolete, another's will."

—THEODORE LEVITT, ECONOMIST, PROFESSOR, AND
FORMER EDITOR OF HARVARD BUSINESS REVIEW[1]

Growing up in Maine, a pair of duck boots from L.L. Bean was almost required winter and mud season wear. Founded in 1912, L.L. Bean differentiated itself through the quality of its products and its guarantees.

"L.L. Bean boots aren't manufactured. They're made," states a promotional video highlighting the very manual stitching process required to produce a pair at the Brunswick, Maine facility, just down the road from where I was raised.[2] All in all, it takes 200 people and 85 minutes of labor to handmake a pair of duck boots.[3]

---

1   Levitt 2008, 36
2   "The Making Of An American Icon" 2019
3   Lam 2015

Contrasting with this image of traditional manual construction was the news in February 2018 that L.L. Bean planned on testing embedding sensor technology into its boots to gather usage data.

"L.L. Bean plans to ship a line of coats and boots with sewn-in sensors that send data to the public Ethereum blockchain platform," reported the *Wall Street Journal*. The concept would be to collect "[d]igital, quantifiable data about how customers are actually using a product," according to L.L. Bean innovation specialist Chad Leeder.[4]

The program would have been small and opt-in, with the purpose of better understanding how products are used and what may lead to their failure.

"If we can see that the customer really is utilizing [a product] in the way we intended, if they're wearing it in the right climate or on a daily basis, that helps us decide whether it's still viable in a market," Leeder said. "If we see a high return rate, we'll analyze why."[5]

Unfortunately, just a month later, the project was canceled.

Sensational media coverage of the project, suggesting that L.L. Bean was about to monitor and track the location of all its boots and their wearers, surely contributed to this decision. "[F]ollowing people around... is unnerving and disturbing... Electronic eyes can traces [sic] your footsteps

---

4   Nash 2018a
5   Ibid.

into the laundry to take note of highly personal habits," cautioned *Inc. Magazine.*[6]

This was a shame. Such data could have helped L.L. Bean understand how its products were being used. This is one of the promises of the Internet of Things (IoT): better data bringing better products.

"If you can't be 100% clear about what information you're collecting and transparently explain what you're going to do with it, you're going to end up on the wrong side of the creepy line," Gartner research director Bart Willemsen said about the debacle.[7]

Separately, part of L.L Bean's allure for over 100 years was its incredible 100% lifetime guarantee. If a customer ever wanted to return a product, they could — no questions asked.

So it came as a shock to many when L.L. Bean radically changed this policy mere days after this blockchain usage reversal. The updated policy would only cover products for a year and require proof of purchase. Beyond that year, the policy would only cover items that had material or craftsmanship defects.[8]

While this is still a generous policy by any standard, it is a marked change. The reason?

---

6   Sherman 2018
7   Nash 2018b
8   "L.L. Bean - Easy Returns And Exchanges" 2019

"Increasingly, a small, but growing number of customers has been interpreting our guarantee well beyond its original intent," executive chairman Shawn Gorman explained via Facebook. "Some view it as a lifetime product replacement program, expecting refunds for heavily worn products used over many years. Others seek refunds for products that have been purchased through third parties, such as at yard sales."[9]

This small group was causing very real damage, however. An MIT Sloan Management Review feature estimated that only 0.4% of customers were "abusive returners" but cost L.L. Bean "$50 million per year, or roughly 30% of the company's annual profits."[10]

Regardless, the abrupt and universal shift in return policy upset many customers. Why couldn't the company target the offending customers and leave the rest alone?

Perhaps L.L. Bean simply lacked the internal data to do so. Ironically, the data that the blockchain project would have collected could have helped. By better understanding how their boots failed, the company could have better understood which returns were legitimate and thus better targeted its return policy.

"If a company can justify clamping down on a customer with a history of questionable return behavior, it can avoid coming under public fire for instituting broad

9   Gorman 2018
10   Abbey, Ketzenberg and Metters 2018

return restrictions — the way L.L. Bean did," wrote the MIT Sloan authors.[11]

* * *

External data monetization is important to consider, but internal use of data to understand your customers is essential. As the L.L. Bean example shows, better data can assist not only in product development but customer service as well, both of which can have a direct effect on the bottom line.

Many companies successfully focus on harnessing data to improve their offerings. Recall how Tesla and Oatly, via control of their channel, are able to create a positive feedback cycle between their customers and product development.

Another example is Blake's Seed Based, a consumer food "microbrand," which began by selling its allergen-free snacks via its own website when it launched in January 2018. "Selling directly to consumers means that microbrands boast a wealth of data," according to *The Economist*. "Their giant rivals, by contrast, use data filtered by retailers."[12]

---

11 Ibid.
12 "The Growth Of Microbrands Threatens Consumer-Goods Giants" 2018

By September of the same year, the company had enough customer data to reformulate and improve its products. Although Blake's Seed Based is now also available via Amazon, the company gained critical feedback and customer loyalty by taking its time with channel partnerships.

Stitch Fix, an e-commerce women's fashion box delivery service, is another that has used data science to understand its customers better and consequently improve its offerings.

Through a product called Style Shuffle, customers rate a variety of clothing each day. "It not only trains the company's algorithm to understand holistically a client's personal style, but it also draws customers back to the app and interests them in Stitch Fix's inventory," reports *Fast Company*. Over 75% of Stitch Fix's clients have used the rating product, giving the company invaluable insights into their customers' preferences.[13]

These are insights that Stitch Fix, in turn, can share with its suppliers. Giving detailed customer feedback information about a supplier's clothing makes Stitch Fix a much more valuable channel partner than traditional retail.

With Style Shuffle and other tools, Stitch Fix is organized in a way that collecting valuable data is natural and unobtrusive to the user while feeding directly back into its product management and channel strategy. "[We] almost

---

13   Smiley 2019

should be paying the customers to do this for us," says chief algorithms officer Eric Colson.[14] A brave admission!

Such data insights are an important part of how industrial companies can utilize their assets, too. According to an article by Vijay Govindarajan of Dartmouth's Tuck School of Business and Jeffrey R. Immelt, former chairperson and CEO of General Electric for 16 years:

> *Manufacturers can create value from the industrial IoT in several ways and should deploy all of them at the same time. By analyzing all the data on how customers are using, maintaining, and repairing their machines, manufacturers can build better-performing products that last longer and require less service. Superior products drive sales, even in flat markets, which will yield more data over time. Thus, market leaders may be able to trigger network effects in hardware sales.*[15]

For many companies, however, the issue is not a lack of data but knowing how to use it.

According to business researchers Jeanne W. Ross, Cynthia M. Beath, and Anne Quaadgras in the *Harvard Business Review*, "most companies don't do a good job with the information they already have. They don't know how to manage it, analyze it in ways that enhance their

---

14 Ibid.
15 Govindarajan and Immelt 2019

understanding, and then make changes in response to new insights."[16]

Amazon successfully uses its data to police users, as L.L. Bean perhaps wishes it could. Despite offering relatively easy returns, Amazon will ban users who seem to be abusing its policies.

"We want everyone to be able to use Amazon, but there are rare occasions where someone abuses our service over an extended period of time," an Amazon spokesman explained to the *Wall Street Journal*. "We never take these decisions lightly, but with over 300 million customers around the world, we take action when appropriate to protect the experience for all our customers.[17]

By operating in a manner that the vast majority of customers see as fair, Amazon is able to maintain its reputation for customer service while removing bad actors.

* * *

Many companies are just at the beginning stages of understanding how better data collection can be fed back into product management and commercial operations. When I speak with clients, they often surprise themselves with how many potential sources of useful data they can

---

16   Ross, Beath and Quaadgras 2013
17   Stevens 2018

name. The problem is in the collection, dissemination, and use of that data to drive better decision making.

Customer-provided data is essential to making sure your company is providing the best value it can.

KEY TAKEAWAYS

- One of the greatest uses of data internally is understanding customers and their preferences better.
- Good data is a critical part of the feedback cycle enabling better service and product development.
- Knowing the customer is essential for every company, and verifying that existing data is being used is critical.

KEY QUESTIONS

- How can you use data already available to better understand your customers?
- How is your company collecting, analyzing, and using customer data to improve its value offering?
- What changes need to be made internally to improve your company's data utilization?

CONCLUSION

CONCLUSION

Chapter 19

TYING IT TOGETHER

"Bad companies are destroyed by crisis. Good companies survive them. Great companies are improved by them."

—ANDY GROVE, FORMER CEO OF INTEL[1]

So far we have been focusing on different revolutions at the intersection of technology and business that are transforming marketplaces faster than at any other point since the Industrial Revolution.

Reintermediation described how innovative companies are finding new ways of providing value in roiling industries. Technology has not destroyed intermediaries; it has empowered new ones to take over. Customers faced with more options than ever often require *more* assistance from intermediaries, not less.

In **Monetization**, we explored how technology is enabling more companies and industries to experiment with their pricing models. There are many options, and the choices a company makes about its pricing strategy

---

1   Holiday 2014, 3

influence, and are influenced by, its decisions about branding and customer interaction.

With **Transparency,** we delineated between price transparency and pricing transparency. Contrary to how many use the terms, they are not synonymous. Higher levels of transparency are neither always better for customers nor always worse for suppliers. We saw how information technology is empowering customers and what opportunities that opens for companies.

Channel dealt with the tumult occurring in traditional distribution networks and the companies that are using technology to reshape customer interactions across entire industries. It asked companies to take a step back and assess whether their channel partners are performing the five channel functions better than other potential partners (or their own company) could. Also, it challenged companies to ensure they are staying close to their customers.

Data showed the monumental importance of data in the digital economy, but also how refining that data into insights enables services to move up the value chain. Issues of monetization are similar to those of non-data services, but also carry unique risks. The most important corporate use of data is better understanding customers and their problems to be solved.

These five revolutions constitute what I call the New Invisible Hand.

In each section, we've seen how certain companies are recognizing the challenges these revolutions bring and figuring out ways to mitigate their risk or, better yet, make the revolutions work *for* their strategy.

As Jeff Bezos has asked: "Are the world's trends tailwinds for you?"[2]

This is not a new world in which only young companies can survive. Many decades-old incumbents are stepping up to the challenge as well, if not better, than the insurgents. We have met some of those incumbents already.

---

2   Bezos 2017

The takeaways and questions at the end of each chapter should give you food for thought as to how well your company is currently addressing the challenges presented. These takeaways may also enable you to see gaps in the market for new opportunities.

Consider these points a starting place for discussion, not a pre-packaged answer. Business strategy cannot be cookie-cutter, and neither can your strategic reactions to these technological revolutions.

Are there overarching themes that unify these forces? Ones that are characteristic of how successful companies are managing incredible changes? And, conversely, ones that companies struggling to stay relevant are missing?

In the following two chapters, I will bring together the intertwining threads of the five sections and show how they point to two imperatives: serving customers well, and serving them profitably.

Chapter 20

FOCUS ON CUSTOMERS

"When you're designing a product or setting a price, don't just think about what customers want, but who they want to be."

—ROGER L. MARTIN, FORMER DIRECTOR OF MONITOR GROUP AND FORMER DEAN OF THE UNIVERSITY OF TORONTO ROTMAN SCHOOL OF MANAGEMENT[1]

In 1993, Michael Treacy and Fred Wiersema published a seminal piece in the *Harvard Business Review* entitled "Customer Intimacy and Other Value Disciplines." Within, they laid out a view that companies must choose and pursue one of the following corporate strategies to deliver value to customers:

- **Operational excellence**: the goal of companies that focus on driving down costs and inconveniences in the buying process. Examples: Craigslist and Dell.
- **Customer intimacy**: the characteristic of companies that truly know their customers and tailor their offerings to

---

1   Martin 2019

match a wide variety of customer interests. Examples:
Amazon and Netflix.

- **Product leadership**: the path demonstrated by companies that are on the cutting edge of innovation and
whose brands are synonymous with first-in-class products. Examples: Apple and Tesla.[2]

According to Treacy and Wiersema:

*Companies that push the boundaries of one value disci-
pline while meeting industry standards in the other two
gain such a lead that competitors find it hard to catch up.
This is largely because the leaders have aligned their entire
operating model—that is, the company's culture, business
processes, management systems, and computer platforms—
to serve one value discipline.[3]*

The framework of operational excellence, customer intimacy, and product leadership is useful. However, there is
a fundamental emerging tenet behind all three thanks to
the New Invisible Hand:

Every company today must focus on the customer, or
be left behind.

* * *

2   Treacy and Wiersema 1993
3   Ibid.

Considering the five revolutions, there is one key role that recurs again and again: the *customer*.

Reintermediation centers on how new forms of value-add are created by companies who find new ways to serve customers in existing marketplaces.

Monetization models can encourage and motivate your customers, or it can alienate them entirely. There is no one right answer; it depends on your customer strategy.

Transparency is increasingly a fact of the marketplace, but how your company addresses it has important implications for how customers interact and respond to its value propositions.

Channel is all about how best to reach and serve your customers. If channel partners are not making it easier for you to understand and sell to your customers, they are destroying value.

Data must be an essential input to improving product innovation and the customer relationship. Misuse of data can ruin trust and sabotage the core business.

The customer is key. Your success in the face of each revolution depends on how well your approach to it works for your customers.

That is why it is so critical for companies to get outside of their own organizations when defining and quantifying value. Internal stakeholders may know everything there is to know about the product and what it can do, but they are not customers. Without knowing what customers actually care about, the team responsible for marketing and selling that product may easily find itself barking up the wrong tree.

Beauty may be in the eye of the beholder, but value is in the eye of the customer. If the customer doesn't perceive or acknowledge the value, it doesn't exist.

If there is value the customer doesn't perceive, that value either must be demonstrated or cannot be part of the value proposition and therefore cannot factor into price. Also, if customers are not accessing all of the relevant value of an offering, then the company is losing out.

Part of customer experience is making sure customers are making good use of your products. "A high performing customer success organization will pay for itself many times over," says Jeff MacMillan, senior director of business models for Autodesk, the multibillion-dollar software company.[4] Companies need to ensure that customers are equipped for success.

As a defining example of operational excellence, Dell's original insight was that it could better serve a large class of personal computer shoppers by foregoing traditional distribution systems. Buyers could customize their PC as well, something that was unheard of at the time. Yes, they succeeded by trimming operational costs, but first

---

4   MacMillan 2019

and foremost by recognizing an unmet customer need and providing a solution.

Product innovation companies must have a crystal clear understanding of their customers as well. Tesla's CEO, Elon Musk, is amazingly available via Twitter and responds directly to customer concerns. When a customer suggested a car in park shift the steering wheel and seat to make it easier to get in and out of the vehicle, Musk responded within 24 minutes with a promise to add such functionality to a future release.

In the words of *Inc. Magazine*, "Attention, all business leaders: This is how to use social media."[5]

This is not to say all companies are actually the same. Apple and Craigslist are very different companies, but both owe their success to being intimately involved with the concerns of their customers.

Every company must be in the business of customer intimacy, even those defined by their operational excellence or product leadership. There is simply no alternative in today's economy.

FINDING YOUR TRUE CUSTOMERS

The imperative to stay close to your customers was highlighted in the Channel and Data revolutions, but is an undercurrent to the others as well. Each trend can be

---

5   Bariso 2017

harnessed to gain a better understanding of what customers want and value.

But who are your customers? That is not always a straightforward question.

For medical devices, there are many different types of users. The buyer may be a hospital or medical group. The direct user could be a doctor or technician. The recipient could be a pediatric patient. The bill payer could be a parent, through an insurance company. All of these players get some value from the product and service. And they all value different things. It is important to understand all of their points of view.

"Your task here is to decide *who you are really creating value for and what they value is*," [emphasis in the original] according to University of Sydney Business School senior lecturer Dr. Massimo Garbuio and Macquarie University Business School senior lecturer Nidthida Lin.[6]

Certain high-growth digital enterprise companies, such as Zoom (video communication) and Slack (communication and productivity), have focused on being incredibly easy for end users to use and therefore driving demand from the bottom up. This contrasts with more mature competitors such as Webex and Microsoft Office, who have been used to appeal to the traditional top-down IT purchase process. But for Zoom, it has worked: 55% of customers

---

6 Garbuio and Lin 2018

that currently spend over $100,000 started with a single user driving demand.[7]

Take the time to understand the entire ecosystem around your products and services. Talk to existing customers and users. Find who you are really creating value for, and how. As much as possible, quantify it.

"Ultimately, it's the focus on customers that makes you successful," Tomas Laboutka, the co-founder of travel intermediary HotelQuickly, told me. As we've learned, such a two-sided platform must attract both sides in order to function, as is the case with other platform examples throughout this book, such as Cars.com and Lyft.

For travelers, HotelQuickly finds last-minute deals on hotels. For hotels, the service helps to fill vacancies and attract new customers. Platform intermediaries that serve both sides of a marketplace need to understand both sides of their customer base to ensure that they are creating value for each.

Some platforms will aggressively target the consumer side of the marketplace to gain users, which then becomes a negotiation tool to acquire more suppliers. But Laboutka first knew he had a winning concept when he started getting traction not only with travelers but with the hotels, as well.

_____

7   Poyar 2019

Instead of hotels feeling obligated to join his service, they were eager to participate because HotelQuickly appealed to both sides of the equation. Both consumers and suppliers, in the end, are interested in making a trade.

"It's ultimately a two-sided marketplace: B2B and B2C. The moment you're gaining supply partners as well as engagement on the side of the customers is the moment you're getting verification," Laboutka told me.

"At the end of the day, the customer wants to have an amazing hotel designed for them at the right price. The hotel wants to sell at the right price," Laboutka said. "The marketplace in between is where the magic happens."

He paused. "Of course, if you're short-sighted, if you're gunning for only one side of it, you are running inevitably into conflict." But the two sides don't necessarily have to conflict, as well-functioning two-sided platforms reveal.

B2B CUSTOMER EXPERIENCE

Thanks to innovations fostered by the Digital Revolution, customer experience expectations are higher than ever. Customers are used to amazing experiences from leading B2C companies, and B2B needs to catch up.

"Our B2C experiences are driving our B2B expectations," states Paul Adair, global director of marketing, inside sales, and customer operations at PolyOne, a global plastics company.[8]

In other words? "Amazon has spoiled us all," according to Stephanie Yee, vice president at food service giant Sysco.[9]

It is worth pausing on Amazon. "Undoubtedly one of the easiest companies to do business with," describes customer experience expert and author Shep Hyken. Amazon "creates confidence at every level," he stresses.[10] This is incredibly valuable.

Amazon's CEO Jeff Bezos is famous for his customer-centricity. As he stated in his 2016 letter to shareholders:

There are many advantages to a customer-centric approach, but here's the big one: customers are always beautifully, wonderfully dissatisfied, even when they report being happy and business is great. Even when they don't yet know it, customers want something better, and your desire to delight customers will drive you to invent on their behalf. No customer ever asked Amazon to create the Prime membership program, but it sure turns out they wanted it... [11]

---

8   Adair 2019
9   Yee 2018
10 Hyken 2019
11 Bezos 2017

The question that every B2B company should especially consider is how to bring this level of service to their industries. There is nothing inherent about B2B that makes the customer experience less important. That is a valuable truth for companies that can capitalize on it.

If a company as large and sprawling as Amazon can be customer-centric, any company can be.

* * *

The importance of customer value is not a new insight. It is a fundamental fact of an economy in which customers have options and freedom.

In turbulent times, it is tempting to look for a new trick or hack to survive for another day. In fact, turbulence is a state in which it is critical to go back to the basics. Providing customer value is the only thing that will earn your company those customers and the profits they bring.

KEY TAKEAWAYS

- Every company must be in the business of customer intimacy to stay relevant.
- Many companies serve more than one type of customer, and all of them are critical to the company's overall value proposition.

- B2B companies in particular have much opportunity to improve (and differentiate themselves from the competition) via the customer experience.

KEY QUESTIONS

- How can your company rise to meet the challenge of constantly increasing customer expectations?
- How can your company use an understanding of each revolution to improve its relationship with customers?
- Which customers has your company been neglecting or losing focus on that are an important part of its ecosystem?

Chapter 21

FOCUS ON PROFITS

"Profits are not a zero sum game. The more you make the more of a financial impact you can have."

—*MARK CUBAN, BUSINESSMAN AND INVESTOR*[1]

The existential purpose of a company is not only serving customers, but doing so profitably. Many observers of the Digital Revolution are concerned that increased digitization and technological change means lower prices and lower profits. How can companies survive in such a new environment?

Disruption from the five revolutions is a matter of fact. But strategic companies can find ways to harness these revolutions to deliver even more value to customers, consequently earning even more profits.

---

1   Cuban 2011

PROFITABILITY IS SUSTAINABILITY

While serving customers' needs is necessary to make a business, it is not sufficient. Businesses must make a profit to survive.

Ride-hailing services, such as Uber and Lyft, have featured positively throughout this book. They are clear manifestations of the technological revolutions we've discussed, and they have excelled at commandeering the imperatives the revolutions demand.

But so far, such services still fail a critical test of what determines a great company: profitability.

Despite all their success, Uber and Lyft remain deeply unprofitable as of 2019. Serious questions remain about whether their models can eventually turn a profit. Until then, customers are being delighted unsustainably on the backs of billions of dollars in investors' capital. That's great for customers while it lasts, but sooner or later investors may come calling.

"The big question is, [ride hailing continues] to be subsidized by investors," says Bloomberg News columnist Matt Levine. "What is the long-term outcome of that?"[2]

He continues:

[Investors'] bet is that the long-term outcome of [ride hailing] is self-driving cars, and that they have some sort of

---

2   "Matt Levine Live At Bloomberg HQ (Ep. 34)" 2019

advantage in being the provider of the self-driving car app, which I'm not sure if that is super compelling because it seems to me it's hard to build a self-driving car. It's relatively easy to build a routing app to send the self-driving car to you.

If Tesla or Apple or whoever built the best self-driving car, I'll download Tesla's app. So it's a risk for Uber.[3]

In China, food delivery services such as Meituan Dianping have been heavily subsidized by investors and are struggling to find a path to profitability. Despite a market capitalization of around $36 billion, analyst Leo Sun of *The Motley Fool* says, "a pricing war will likely prevent Meituan from becoming profitable for the foreseeable future."[4]

Ride-hailing services could find profitability through deploying their learnings to higher margin activities, cutting out costly human drivers, or simply raising fares. After years of slugging it out on market share, we are in fact seeing fares rise according to Lyft's IPO filing.[5] But if low prices are a key part of their current popularity, there may not be sufficient wiggle room on fares to bring the profitability investors seek.

---

3   Ibid.
4   Huang 2019
5   Brown 2019

"Until they turn profits, ride-hailing firms will be vulnerable to a loss of investors' patience," cautions *The Economist*.[6]

Airbnb, on the other hand, has reached profitability for two years running.[7] Tesla had a couple profitable quarters in 2018, but is wavering as of this book's publication.[8] Investors, of course, are looking for eventual profitability out of any investment.

In this area in particular, established companies may have a certain leg up on disruptive startups. They are used to the discipline imposed by profitability expectations.

The week that Sears declared bankruptcy, Walmart CEO Doug McMillon stated in an interview that his company was focused on "becoming a digital company, and other things than how to be a brick-and-mortar retail store."[9]

Walmart is challenging Amazon, its major retail competition, by having purchased Jet.com for its e-commerce strength, signing deals with Google's Waymo autonomous vehicles unit, testing autonomous delivery robots with Fedex, and promising one-day delivery to compete directly with Amazon Prime, to name a few initiatives.[10]

---

6   "Riding Alone In A Car Is A Luxury—An Increasingly Unaffordable One" 2019

7   Dickey 2019

8   Ferris 2019

9   Ferriss 2018

10   Sozzi 2019

Powerful, battle-worn incumbents with strategic vision are not simply going to lie down.

Profitability enables companies to improve, grow, and increase shareholder value. It causes the economy to expand.

Management legend Peter Drucker wrote in 1963, "There is surely nothing quite so useless as doing with great efficiency what should not be done at all."[11]

If a business model fundamentally cannot turn a profit, those business activities should not be done. They are actively destroying value.

AVOIDING A RACE TO THE BOTTOM

"Everybody thinks that the race is to zero. That's a stupid race to run." Lynn Guinn of Cargill laughed. "You don't want to be a part of that race. You want to run to the higher ground, not lower ground. You want to figure out how to make more money, not less."

One of the benefits of focusing on the customer is that it allows companies to sell on value, not price. When the focus is on value, the benefits of the product become more important than the price. By starting with the customer and working backwards to the product, you avoid the risk of a race to the bottom.

---

11   Drucker 1963

Emphasizing price teaches your customers they should pay attention to your price, rather than the value your product delivers. Competing on price tends to drive prices down, and therefore drives margins down too.

Competing on low price is a tough path. If your products are similar to your competitors', then the only way you can win a price war is to have a lower cost of production and service than your competitors. There can only be one company with the lowest cost, and the companies that manage cost really well tend to establish large networks that are hard to overturn. As a retailer, do you really want to compete head-on with Amazon and Walmart?

Only one company can have the lowest price for a given product or service. Having different products and services, in other words differentiation, is the best way to compete.

It can be hard to remember now, but when Uber launched as a black car service, it cost well more than a typical taxi. It was not competing with taxis on price, but on service. As then-CEO Travis Kalanick described his company: "The luxury of Uber is about time and convenience."[12]

Many of the companies featured in the Channel section have succeeded by looking upmarket. Tesla and Oatly, for example, are not mass market products. They are high-value and appeal to a limited set of customers. Because

---

12   Stone 2017, 185

of that customer focus, both companies can eschew traditional distribution. Tesla saves enormously on the cost of dealerships. Oatly avoided the bloodbath of the grocery aisle.

"If business leaders see only margin erosion in their future, they aren't thinking big enough," Guinn concluded.

Find points of differentiation. If you can't find any, create them.

MAKE PRICING WORK FOR YOU

When I first began consulting, I was surprised how much of pricing is getting people to care less about price.

If your pricing model doesn't align with the value you are creating, it causes friction in the commercial process. Pricing becomes first and foremost on customers' minds when interacting with you.

This is doubly true for companies that rely too heavily on discounts and rebates. Excessive price concessions are a great way to train your customers that they should focus on your price rather than on value created.

Think of the last mailing you received from the local grocery store. It probably contained all sorts of promotions for various products, announcing in large block numbers what the discount of the week was. What were these ads asking you to focus on: the product or the price?

As marketing guru Seth Godin has written: "Perhaps the reason price is all your customers care about is because you haven't given them anything else to care about."[13]

Pricing strategy should make pricing nearly invisible. A good pricing model should focus customer attention on what they're getting. A bad pricing model focuses customer attention on what they're paying.

In the Transparency revolution, we saw how Careem uses clear communication about pricing to assuage customers' concerns and make their purchasing decisions easier. An informative yet unobtrusive presentation of price reduces uncertainty and increases conversion. While being agreeably transparent, Careem has made its pricing less of a sticking point.

We learned in Monetization how more complex pricing arrangements can also be a hindrance to sales. Conversely, as is the case with Southwest Airlines or Groupon, simplified pricing can be a competitive advantage. The tradeoff between complexity and ease of use must be resolved individually by every company in a way that supports its larger corporate strategy.

---

13 Manning 2012

LOOK FOR NEW SOLUTIONS

Technological innovation opens up new ways to solve problems, both already existing and heretofore unimagined. The first step here is simply to pay attention.

Cars.com brought classified advertising to the digital world, solving the same dealer customer needs (e.g., local marketing) as well as completely new ones (e.g., collecting and distributing leads of potential shoppers). They and others in the area have made very profitable businesses in the meantime.

Ride-hailing companies such as Uber and Lyft found an entirely new way to solve the customer problem of urban transportation. The need already existed, but the means by which to solve it depended on certain technological developments. Now, such companies are working on using their networks and data to provide more solutions.

Recalling Chapter 12: Highlighting Value, put your customer at the forefront of your product innovation process and get pricing involved early. Make it a habit.

"You can systematize innovation even if you can't completely predict it," says former executive chairman of Google and Alphabet Eric Schmidt.[14]

Find something nobody thinks about, and think about it.

---

14   Ferriss 2019

KEY TAKEAWAYS

- Even with the Digital Revolution, sooner or later, businesses must find a path to profitability.

- Technological disruption doesn't have to mean a race to zero margin. Look for opportunities to go upmarket.

- Involving pricing earlier in the product innovation cycle can help ensure the existence of a profitable market for new offerings.

KEY QUESTIONS

- How is your company's pricing model helping to make it easy for customers to buy?

- Are there upmarket opportunities for your company that aren't being realized?

- How is your company systematizing its product innovation to design offerings for profitability?

Chapter 22

PARTING THOUGHTS

"The best way to predict the future is to create it."

—*PETER DRUCKER, PIONEERING*
MANAGEMENT CONSULTANT[1]

The Digital Revolution has unleashed incredible changes in the business landscape via reintermediation, monetization, transparency, channel, and data. They constitute the New Invisible Hand, which is transforming how markets, industries, and individual companies create and deliver value. Now that you know how to identify these trends, you will start to notice their effects everywhere you look.

While we cannot control these five revolutions, we can choose to see our reality as one of opportunity, rather than crisis. A rapidly changing business landscape is one in which the customers and profits are there for those who act. This book has featured many executives and companies that are doing just that.

---

1   Williamson 1986, 149

When I think of the opportunities afforded by these revolutions, I cannot wait to see how companies continue to capitalize on them. Every year, entrepreneurs and forward-thinking executives create brilliant new products and services, and think up new ways to bring them to customers.

It is contingent upon existing mature companies to decide how best to stay on top of such dynamics. Which corporate powerhouses of today will weather the changes? Which will crumble suddenly or simply diminish into irrelevancy?

Having his career in the age of Avis, my grandfather couldn't see how a concept like Zipcar could ever be successful. The logistics and technology required, not to mention the shifts in consumer expectations, were too far removed from his experience.

The first time I experienced the internet was in fourth grade when a teacher showed us the website for the White House. I graduated college just in time for the Great Recession. The concept of using digital technology to drive places without needing to buy a car therefore made sense to me and was comfortable to use.

Zipcar, in turn, has been heavily disrupted by ride-hailing services. When I first sat in an Uber, I could never have imagined how quickly and forcefully it would transform the experience of moving around in a city. The idea wasn't immediately intuitive to me, but I became a regular user as its value became clear.

My daughter is six months old. By the time she is in high school, the idea of using a smartphone to hail a car with a human driver may seem terribly quaint. Already, autonomous vehicles are on the streets. And ride-hailing services are racing against each other to deliver whatever will be the next manifestation of personal transportation, and whatever other customer needs their tools and learnings enable them to address.

I wonder what the technological and business landscape will look like when she grows up. Companies discussed in this book are going to create incredible developments, and companies not yet founded will be groundbreaking in ways we cannot imagine.

We can't predict the future. So, in the words of Jeff Bezos: "Focus on the things that don't change."[2]

The concept of the New Invisible Hand presents a framework for thriving in this rapidly changing world. We can't know what technologies will define tomorrow. But we can understand the forces that are bringing the future closer every day and the principles that matter more than ever.

I look forward to hearing about your adventures navigating our increasingly dynamic business landscape.

---

2   Haden 2017

ACKNOWLEDGMENTS

Thank you to my parents and siblings for their love and encouragement in my creative and professional endeavors. Also to extended family, present and past. You all, in short, have made me who I am today.

Thank you to my wife and daughter for your support throughout this project. Also, for your patience and understanding when writing and editing kept me late in the basement.

Thank you to all of my interviewees. Those who didn't make it by name into the final publication were still essential in focusing and prioritizing material. This book is a co-creation with you all.

Thank you to my advance readers, Prof. Cheng Gao, Prof. Zafar Iqbal, Lynn Nguyen, and Haley Van Lahr. Your astute eyes helped to clarify points, remove chaff, and make for a much stronger book.

Thank you to my colleagues at Wiglaf Pricing, especially Tim J. Smith, Jeanette Gerger, and Nathan Phipps. Working with you is a pleasure.

Finally, thank you to Prof. Eric Koester and everyone at New Degree Press for your guidance and hard work in bringing this book across the finish line.

BIBLIOGRAPHY

INTRODUCTION

"Industrial Revolution". 2019. *Encyclopedia Britannica*. https://www.britannica.com/event/Industrial-Revolution.

Marcec, Dan. 2018. "CEO Tenure Rates". *Corpgov.Law.Harvard. Edu*. https://corpgov.law.harvard.edu/2018/02/12/ceo-tenure-rates/.

Mochari, Ilan. 2016. "Why Half Of The S&P 500 Companies Will Be Replaced In The Next Decade". *Inc.Com*. https://www.inc.com/ilan-mochari/innosight-sp-500-new-companies.html.

OECD Secretariat. 2018. "Market Concentration". Organisation for Economic Co-operation and Development. https://one.oecd.org/document/DAF/COMP/WD(2018)46/en/pdf.

Primack, Dan. 2011. "Zoom, zoom: Zipcar is a $1 billion company!". *Fortune*. http://fortune.com/2011/04/14/zoom-zoom-zipcar-is-a-1-billion-company/.

"Quotation of the Day". 2005. *The New York Times.* https://www.nytimes.com/2005/07/12/nyregion/quotation-of-the-day.html.

"Sam Altman On Loving Community, Hating Coworking, And The Hunt For Talent (Ep. 61—Live)". 2019. *Medium.* https://medium.com/conversations-with-tyler/tyler-cowen-sam-altman-ai-tech-business-58f530417522.

Schawbel, Dan. 2012. "How Robin Chase Reinvented The Transportation Industry". *Forbes.com.* https://www.forbes.com/sites/danschawbel/2012/06/22/how-robin-chase-rein-vented-the-transportation-industry/.

Sheetz, Michael. 2017. "Technology Killing Off Corporate America: Average Life Span Of Companies Under 20 Years". *CNBC.* https://www.cnbc.com/2017/08/24/technol-ogy-killing-off-corporations-average-lifespan-of-compa-ny-under-20-years.html.

Smith, Adam. 1937. *An Inquiry Into The Nature And Causes Of The Wealth Of Nations.* New York: Random House, Inc.

Sweetwood, Matt. 2018. "Infographic: The 20 Most Common Reasons Startups Fail And How To Avoid Them". *Entrepreneur.* https://www.entrepreneur.com/article/307724.

"Zipcar Overview | Zipcar Press Center". 2019. *Zipcar.com.*
https://www.zipcar.com/press/overview.

I. REINTERMEDIATION

CHAPTER 1. THE BIRTH OF REINTERMEDIATION

Ballentine, Lee. 2014. "What Is The Percentage Of Books Published On Which Publishers Actually Lose Money?". *Forbes.
Com.* https://www.forbes.com/sites/quora/2014/05/28/
what-is-the-percentage-of-books-published-on-which-pub-
lishers-actually-lose-money/.

Fallows, James. 2004. "TECHNO FILES; The Twilight Of
The Information Middlemen". *Nytimes.Com.* https://www.
nytimes.com/2004/05/16/business/techno-files-the-twi-
light-of-the-information-middlemen.html.

Gates, Bill, Paul Allen, Brent Schlender, and Henry Gold-
blatt. 1995. "Bill Gates & Paul Allen Talk Check Out The
Ultimate Buddy Act in Business History: The Multibil-
lionaire Co-Founders Of Microsoft Sit Still For An Entire
Afternoon To Tell Fortune's Brent Schlender Their Story
And Speculate About The Future Of Personal Computing
And Telecommunications - October 2, 1995". *Archive.For-
tune.Com.* http://archive.fortune.com/magazines/fortune/
fortune_archive/1995/10/02/206528/index.htm.

Hagiu, Andrei, and Elizabeth J. Altman. 2017. "Is There A Platform In Your Product?". *Harvard Business Review*. https://hbr.org/2017/07/finding-the-platform-in-your-product.

"Imagining The Internet". 2019. *Elon.Edu*. http://www.elon.edu/predictions/prediction2.aspx?id=JAG-0053.

Lohr, Steve. 1997. "Profiting As A Business-To-Business Middleman On The Internet Is Tricky.". *Nytimes.Com*. https://www.nytimes.com/1997/05/19/business/profiting-as-a-business-to-business-middleman-on-the-internet-is-tricky.html.

Krakovsky, Marina. 2015a. "In Defense Of The Middleman". *Fast Company*. https://www.fastcompany.com/3049277/in-defense-of-the-middleman.

Krakovsky, Marina. 2015b. *The Middleman Economy: How Brokers, Agents, Dealers, And Everyday Matchmakers Create Value And Profit*. 1st ed. Palgrave Macmillan.

Malik, Om. 2014. "A Few Accumulated Thoughts On Media". *On My Om*. https://om.co/2014/04/14/a-few-accumulated-thoughts-on-media/.

Titcomb, James. 2015. "Windows 95 At 20: How Bill Gates' Software Changed The World". *Telegraph.Co.Uk*. https://www.

telegraph.co.uk/technology/microsoft/windows/11817065/
Twenty-years-ago-Microsoft-launched-Windows-95-chang-
ing-the-world.html.

Venter, Craig. 2008. "Transcript Of "On The Verge Of Creating Synthetic Life"". *Ted.Com*. https://www.ted.com/talks/
craig_venter_is_on_the_verge_of_creating_synthetic_life/
transcript.

CHAPTER 2. INNOVATING ON
TRADITIONAL INTERMEDIARIES

Carson, Biz. 2019. "Lyft'S Revenue Doubled In 2018 As It
Gains On Uber In U.S., But Losses Still Growing". *Forbes.
Com*. https://www.forbes.com/sites/bizcarson/2019/03/01/
its-official-lyft-files-to-go-public/.

"Daily Deals Sites Industry In The US". 2019. *Ibisworld.Com*.
https://www.ibisworld.com/industry-trends/special-
ized-market-research-reports/online-retail/lifestyle-ser-
vices/daily-deals-sites.html.

"Driver And Passenger Ratings". 2019. *Lyft Help*. https://help.
lyft.com/hc/en-us/articles/115013079948-Driver-and-pas-
senger-ratings.

"Estimated Advertising And Circulation Revenue Of The
Newspaper Industry". 2018. *Pew Research Center's Jour-
nalism Project.* https://www.journalism.org/chart/
sotnm-newspapers-newspaper-industry-estimated-ad-
vertising-and-circulation-revenue/.

"Groupon Head Andrew Mason: 'We've Succeeded In Making Coupons Cool'". 2012. *SPIEGEL ONLINE.* https://www.
spiegel.de/international/business/groupon-head-andrew-
mason-we-ve-succeeded-in-making-coupons-cool-a-811405.
html.

Ingram, Mathew. 2013. "Two Charts That Tell You Everything
You Need To Know About The Future Of Newspapers".
Gigaom.Com. https://gigaom.com/2013/04/11/two-charts-
that-tell-you-everything-you-need-to-know-about-the-fu-
ture-of-newspapers/.

Lam, Bourree. 2016. "Who Uses A Travel Agent In This Day
And Age?". *The Atlantic.* https://www.theatlantic.com/
business/archive/2016/06/travel-agent/488282/.

"Michael Munger On Sharing, Transaction Costs, And Tomorrow 3.0". 2018. *Econlib.* http://www.econtalk.org/michael-
munger-on-sharing-transaction-costs-and-tomorrow-3-0/.

Rodriguez, Salvador. 2013. "Lyft, A Ride-Sharing App Service, Expands To Chicago". *Latimes.Com.* https://www.latimes.com/business/technology/la-fi-tn-lyft-chicago-name-change-20130509-story.html.

Sorrells, Mitra. 2018. "Booking Holdings Reveals $12.7B Revenue, Goes Lukewarm On Airbnb Threat | Phocuswire". *Phocuswire.Com.* https://www.phocuswire.com/Booking-Holdings-earnings-full-year-2017.

"Travel Agents: Occupational Outlook Handbook". 2019. *Bureau Of Labor Statistics, U.S. Department Of Labor.* https://www.bls.gov/ooh/sales/travel-agents.htm#tab-1.

"Trends And Facts On Newspapers | State Of The News Media". 2018. *Pew Research Center's Journalism Project.* https://www.journalism.org/fact-sheet/newspapers/.

Weber, Thomas E., and Andrea Petersen. 1999. "Priceline's Initial Public Offering turns Founder Into Billionaire". *WSJ.* https://www.wsj.com/articles/SB922927682927802935.

CHAPTER 3. REINTERMEDIATION OF DIGITAL INTERMEDIARIES

Dallke, Jim. 2018. "As Reverb'S Office Expands, It'S Eyeing Even Bigger Plans For Growth". *American Inno.* https://

www.americaninno.com/chicago/inno-news-chicago/
as-reverbs-office-expands-its-eyeing-even-bigger-plans-
for-growth/.

Davidson, John. 2016. "Black Market Ride-Sharing
Explodes In Austin". *The Federalist*. https://thefederalist.
com/2016/05/23/black-market-ride-sharing-uber-lyft/.

Denning, Steve. 2015. "Fresh Insights From Clayton Christensen On Disruptive Innovation". *Forbes.Com*. https://
www.forbes.com/sites/stevedenning/2015/12/02/fresh-in-
sights-from-clayton-christensen-on-disruptive-innova-
tion/.

Foster, Tom. 2017. "The Brilliant Way One Founder Made A
Killing From The Music Industry". *Inc.Com*. https://www.
inc.com/magazine/201709/tom-foster/2017-inc5000-reverb.
html.

Hodges, Cassie. 2017. "Serial Entrepreneur Scott Case
On Failure, Financing And Flexibility". *Free Enterprise*. https://www.freeenterprise.com/serial-entrepre-
neur-scott-case-failure-financing-flexibility/.

J, Matt. 2018. "How Am I Protected If I Do Not Receive
An Item Or The Item I Receive Is Not As Described?".

Reverb Help Center. https://help.reverb.com/hc/en-us/articles/360003063773.

Jamieson, Dan. 2011. "Schwab Closes On Optionsxpress". *Investmentnews.Com*. https://www.investmentnews.com/article/20110901/FREE/110909994/schwab-closes-on-optionsxpress.

Jopson, Barney. 2012. "The Bezos Doctrine Of Ruthless Pragmatism | Financial Times". *Ft.Com*. https://www.ft.com/content/2398876a-c202-11e1-8e7c-00144feabdc0.

Korosec, Kirsten. 2016. "Priceline Founder Launches New Company Aimed At Business Travelers". *Fortune*. http://fortune.com/2016/06/21/priceline-jay-walker-upside/.

Naughton, Keith, and David Welch. 2019. "This Is What Peak Car Looks Like". *Bloomberg.Com*. https://www.bloomberg.com/news/features/2019-02-28/this-is-what-peak-car-looks-like.

Owens, Jeremy C. 2018. "Amazon Was Almost Worth $1 Trillion, But It Is Down $119 Billion In Just Two Trading Sessions". *Marketwatch*. https://www.marketwatch.com/story/microsoft-on-track-to-pass-amazon-in-market-cap-after-earnings-reports-2018-10-25.

"Reedsy | Crunchbase". 2019. *Crunchbase.* https://www.crunch-base.com/organization/reedsy.

Stone, Brad. 2013. *The Everything Store: Jeff Bezos And The Age Of Amazon.* Little, Brown and Company.

Sun, Leo. 2019. "A Foolish Take: Only 3% Of Millennials Don't Use Amazon". *The Motley Fool.* https://www.fool.com/investing/2019/03/25/a-foolish-take-only-3-of-millennials-dont-use-amaz.aspx.

CHAPTER 4. WHAT'S NEXT

"A Disciplined Startup Emerges From The Wild West Of Crypto-Currency". 2018. *The Economist.* https://www.economist.com/business/2018/06/28/a-disciplined-startup-emerges-from-the-wild-west-of-crypto-currency.

"Amazon Business Sr. Vendor Manager: Tools And Agriculture". 2019. *Linkedin.* Accessed June 14. https://www.linkedin.com/jobs/view/amazon-business-sr-vendor-manager-tools-and-agriculture-at-amazon-970951468/.

"America's Largest Private Companies". 2018. *Forbes.Com.* https://www.forbes.com/largest-private-companies/list/.

Andreessen, Marc. 2011. "Why Software Is Eating The World".
WSJ. https://www.wsj.com/articles/SB10001424053111903
4809045765122509156294.60.

"Andreessen Horowitz". 2019. *Andreessen Horowitz.* Accessed
June 14. https://a16z.com/.

Anthony, Scott D. 2016. "Kodak'S Downfall Wasn'T About
Technology". *Harvard Business Review.* https://hbr.
org/2016/07/kodaks-downfall-wasnt-about-technology.

Arrieta, Jose. 2018. In *Transforming Government, Industry And
Commerce One Blockchain At A Time: The MIT Enterprise
Forum Of Washington, DC & Baltimore.*

"Ben Thompson On Business And Tech (Ep. 52)". 2018.
Medium. https://medium.com/conversations-with-tyler/
ben-thompson-tyler-cowen-stratechery-amazon-goo-
gle-facebook-4bd230276a14.

"Blockchain Expert Explains One Concept In 5 Levels Of Diffi-
culty | WIRED". 2017. *Youtube.* https://www.youtube.com/
watch?v=hYip_Vuv8Jo.

Demery, Paul. 2018. "Q&A: Inside Amazon Business With
Martin Rohde". *Digital Commerce 360.* https://www.dig-

italcommerce360.com/2018/05/02/qa-inside-amazon-business-with-martin-rohde/.

Fortney, Luke. 2019. "Blockchain, Explained". *Investopedia.* https://www.investopedia.com/terms/b/blockchain.asp.

Gao, Cheng, Tiona Zuzul, Geoffrey Jones, and Tarun Khanna. 2017. *Overcoming Institutional Voids: A Reputation-Based View Of Long Run Survival.* Ebook. Harvard Business School. http://www.hbs.edu/faculty/Publication%20Files/17-060_9db63930-4475-4eb5-ac48-a660e2d80690.pdf.

Gupta, Vinay. 2017. "The Promise Of Blockchain Is A World Without Middlemen". *Harvard Business Review.* https://hbr.org/2017/03/the-promise-of-blockchain-is-a-world-without-middlemen.

Morris, Chris. 2019. "Cryptocurrency Owners Can't Access Funds After Exchange CEO Dies—Because No One Knows The Password". *Fortune.* http://fortune.com/2019/02/04/cryptocurrency-quadrigacx-gerald-cotten-frozen-funds/.

Munger, Michael C. 2018. *Tomorrow 3.0: Transaction Costs And The Sharing Economy.* New York: Cambridge University Press.

Parker, Mario, and Javier Blas. 2018. "America'S Largest Private Company Reboots A 153-Year-Old Strategy". *Bloomberg.Com*. https://www.bloomberg.com/news/articles/2018-06-07/america-s-largest-private-company-reboots-a-153-year-old-strategy.

Post, Jennifer. 2019. "What Is Amazon Business And What Are The Benefits To Using It?". *Business News Daily*. https://www.businessnewsdaily.com/9637-what-is-amazon-business.html.

Sheetz, Michael. 2019. "There's A Business Growing Within Amazon That Could One Day Be Worth More Than Retail Or Cloud". *CNBC*. https://www.cnbc.com/2019/03/19/amazon-business-could-be-worth-more-than-core-retail-e-commerce.html.

Vanian, Jonathan. 2018. "Why This 153-Year-Old Company Is Interested In Satellites And A.I.". *Fortune*. http://fortune.com/2018/09/24/cargill-satellites-ai-reinvent/.

II. MONETIZATION

CHAPTER 5. STATIC PRICES

Farfan, Barbara. 2018. "Does Apple Use Discounts, Deals Or Promotions To Sell Apple Products?". *The Balance Small*

Business. https://www.thebalancesmb.com/apple-deals-promotions-2891801.

Ferriss, Tim. 2018. "The Tim Ferriss Show Transcripts: Seth Godin (#343)". *The Blog Of Author Tim Ferriss.* https://tim.blog/2018/11/05/the-tim-ferriss-show-transcripts-seth-godin/.

Meehan, Julie, Mike Simonetto, Larry Montan, and Chris Goodin. 2011. *Pricing And Profitability Management: A Practical Guide For Business Leaders.* 1st ed. Wiley.

Mehta, Neel, Parth Detroja, and Aditya Agashe. 2018. "Amazon Changes Prices On Its Products About Every 10 Minutes — Here's How And Why They Do It". *Business Insider.* https://www.businessinsider.com/amazon-price-changes-2018-8.

CHAPTER 6. VARIABLE PRICING

Gapper, John. 2011. "Lunch With The FT: Howard Schultz". *Ft.Com.* https://www.ft.com/content/04ac1236-50e3-11e0-8931-00144feab49a.

Levitt, Theodore. 1986. *The Marketing Imagination.* New York: The Free Press.

Mattioli, Dana. 2012. "On Orbitz, Mac Users Steered To Pricier Hotels". *WSJ*. https://www.wsj.com/articles/SB100014240 5270230445860457748882267325882.

Valentino-DeVries, Jennifer, Jeremy Singer-Vine, and Ashkan Soltani. 2012. "Websites Vary Prices, Deals Based On Users' Information". *WSJ*. https://www.wsj.com/articles/ SB10001424127887323777204578189391813881534.

CHAPTER 7. INDIVIDUALIZED PRICING

Borison, Rebecca. 2015. "Should Online Retailers Be Charging Different Prices For Same Product?". *Thestreet*. https:// www.thestreet.com/story/13039379/1/should-amazon-be-charging-different-prices-for-same-product.html.

"Episode 633: The Birth And Death Of The Price Tag". 2015. *Planet Money : NPR*. https://www.npr.org/templates/transcript/transcript.php?storyId=415287577.

Kukura, Joe. 2017. "Uber Admits To Manipulating Fares And Prices". *SF Weekly*. http://www.sfweekly.com/news/ uber-admits-manipulating-fares-and-prices/.

Mohammed, Rafi. 2017. "How Retailers Use Personalized Prices To Test What You'Re Willing To Pay". *Harvard*

Business Review. https://hbr.org/2017/10/how-retailers-use-personalized-prices-to-test-what-youre-willing-to-pay.

Obermiller, Carl, David Arnesen, and Marc Cohen. 2012. "Customized Pricing: Win-Win Or End Run?". *Drake Management Review* 1 (2). http://faculty.cbpa.drake.edu/dmr/0102/DMR010204R.pdf.

Tanner, Adam. 2014. "Different Customers, Different Prices, Thanks To Big Data". *Forbes.Com*. https://www.forbes.com/sites/adamtanner/2014/03/26/different-customers-different-prices-thanks-to-big-data/.

Turow, Joseph, Lauren Feldman, and Kimberly Meltzer. 2005. "Open To Exploitation: America's Shoppers Online And Offline". *A Report From The Annenberg Public Policy Center Of The University Of Pennsylvania*. https://repository.upenn.edu/asc_papers/35/.

Walker, Tim. 2017. "How Much ...? The Rise Of Dynamic And Personalised Pricing". *The Guardian*. https://www.theguardian.com/global/2017/nov/20/dynamic-personalised-pricing.

Wallheimer, Brian. 2018. "Are You Ready For Personalized Pricing?". *Chicago Booth Review*. http://review.chicago-

booth.edu/marketing/2018/article/are-you-ready-person-
alized-pricing.

CHAPTER 8. DYNAMIC PRICING

Bhattacharyya, Suman. 2019. "Pressured By Amazon, Retailers Are Experimenting With Dynamic Pricing". *Digiday.*
https://digiday.com/retail/amazon-retailers-experiment-
ing-dynamic-pricing/.

Fussell, Sidney. 2018. "Movie Theater Chain Kills Uber-Style
Surge Pricing After Internet Backlash". *Gizmodo.Com.*
https://gizmodo.com/movie-theater-chain-kills-uber-style-
surge-pricing-afte-1821787911.

Hayes, Dade. 2017. "Should Dynamic Pricing Come To The
Megaplex? Regal Plans Tests In 2018". *Deadline.* https://
deadline.com/2017/10/regal-plans-surge-pricing-movie-
tests-2018-1202194773/.

Hays, Constance. 1999. "Variable-Price Coke Machine Being
Tested". *The New York Times.* https://www.nytimes.
com/1999/10/28/business/variable-price-coke-machine-
being-tested.html.

"How Uber's Dynamic Pricing Model Works". 2019. *Uber Blog.*
https://www.uber.com/en-GB/blog/uber-dynamic-pricing/.

Leonhardt, David. 2005. "Why Variable Pricing Fails At The Vending Machine". *The New York Times*. https://www. nytimes.com/2005/06/27/business/why-variable-pricing-fails-at-the-vending-machine.html.

Mehta, Neel, Parth Detroja, and Aditya Agashe. 2018. "Amazon Changes Prices On Its Products About Every 10 Minutes — Here's How And Why They Do It". *Business Insider*. https://www.businessinsider.com/amazon-price-changes-2018-8.

Morris, Chris. 2017. "Regal Cinemas May Start Charging Less For Flops—And More For Hits". *Fortune*. http://fortune.com/2017/10/25/regal-cinemas-ticket-prices/.

Schechner, Sam. 2017. "Why Do Gas Station Prices Constantly Change? Blame The Algorithm". *WSJ*. https://www.wsj.com/articles/why-do-gas-station-prices-constantly-change-blame-the-algorithm-1494262674.

Shartsis, Alexander. 2019. "Council Post: Dynamic Pricing: The Secret Weapon Used By The World's Most Successful Companies". *Forbes.Com*. https://www.forbes.com/sites/forbestechcouncil/2019/01/08/dynamic-pricing-the-secret-weapon-used-by-the-worlds-most-successful-companies/#e16e83a168ba.

"What Is Dynamic Pricing?". 2019. *Uber Rider Help*. https://
help.uber.com/riders/article/what-is-dynamic-pricing?no-
deId=ba2b4925-9aed-48de-9398-8889607ee0e4.

"Why Are Prices Higher Than Normal?". 2019. *Uber Rider
Help*. https://help.uber.com/riders/article/why-are-prices-
higher-than-normal---?nodeId=34212e8b-d69a-4d8a-a923-
095d3075b487.

CHAPTER 9. SUBSCRIPTION
AND METERED PRICING

Association of Equipment Manufacturers. 2019. "Renting Vs.
Buying: What To Consider Before Your Next Equipment
Purchase". *Pumper*. https://www.pumper.com/online_
exclusives/2019/03/renting-vs-buying-what-to-consider-
before-your-next-equipment-purchase.

Cao, Jing, and Melissa Mittelman. 2016. "Why Unilever Really
Bought Dollar Shave Club". *Bloomberg.Com*. https://www.
bloomberg.com/news/articles/2016-07-20/why-unilever-
really-bought-dollar-shave-club.

Chen, Tony, Ken Fenyo, Sylvia Yang, and Jessica Zhang. 2018.
"Thinking Inside The Subscription Box: New Research
On E-Commerce Consumers". *Mckinsey & Company*.
https://www.mckinsey.com/industries/high-tech/our-in-

sights/thinking-inside-the-subscription-box-new-re-search-on-ecommerce-consumers.

Gabaix, Xavier, and David Laibson. 2006. "Shrouded Attributes, Consumer Myopia, And Information Suppression In Competitive Markets". *The Quarterly Journal Of Economics* 121 (2): 506. https://academic.oup.com/qje/issue/121/2.

Govindarajan, Vijay, and Jeffrey R. Immelt. 2019. "The Only Way Manufacturers Can Survive". *MIT Sloan Management Review.* https://sloanreview.mit.edu/article/the-only-way-manufacturers-can-survive.

"How Food And Beverage Companies Save On Film And Paper Banding". 2015. *Manufacturing.Net.* https://www.manufacturing.net/article/2015/10/how-food-and-beverage-companies-save-film-and-paper-banding.

Isaac, Mike. 2014. "Where Profit Margins Are Hefty, Online Upstarts Muscle In". *The New York Times.* https://www.nytimes.com/2014/09/24/technology/24shave.html.

Lashinsky, Adam. 2015. "How Dollar Shave Club Got Started". *Fortune.* http://fortune.com/2015/03/10/dollar-shave-club-founding/.

"On Point Biz Jets - Details". 2019. *Geaviation.Com*. https://www.geaviation.com/onpointbizjets/details.

Poulter, Sean. 2009. "Sharp Practice? The Razor Heads That Cost Just 5P To Make, But Sell For £2.43 Each". *Daily Mail Online*. https://www.dailymail.co.uk/news/article-1191456/Sharp-practice-The-razor-heads-cost-just-5p-make-sell-2-43-each.html.

Powell, Rose. 2015. "Salesforce Survived Dotcom Crash As Customers Died Around It". *The Sydney Morning Herald*. https://www.smh.com.au/business/salesforce-cofounder-parker-harris-survived-the-dotcom-crash-as-customers-died-around-them-20151004-gk1200.html.

"Pricing". 2019. *Amazon Web Services, Inc.*. https://aws.amazon.com/pricing/.

Protalinski, Emil. 2019. "Microsoft Reports $30.6 Billion In Q3 2019 Revenue: Azure Up 73%, Surface Up 21%, And Linkedin Up 27%". *Venturebeat*. https://venturebeat.com/2019/04/24/microsoft-earnings-q3-2019/.

Rapolu, Bhoopathi. 2016. "Internet Of Aircraft Things: An Industry Set To Be Transformed". *Aviationweek.Com*. https://aviationweek.com/connected-aerospace/internet-aircraft-things-industry-set-be-transformed.

"Rolls-Royce Celebrates 50Th Anniversary Of Power-By-The-Hour". 2012. *Rolls-Royce.Com.* https://www.rolls-royce.com/media/press-releases-archive/yr-2012/121030-the-hour.aspx.

"Self-Driving Cars Will Require New Business Models". 2018. *The Economist.* https://www.economist.com/special-report/2018/03/01/self-driving-cars-will-require-new-business-models.

Thompson, Ben. 2019. "Microsoft, Slack, Zoom, And The Saas Opportunity". *Stratechery.* https://stratechery.com/2019/microsoft-slack-zoom-and-the-saas-opportunity/.

Trefis Team. 2019. "Salesforce.Com To Post $13 Billion+ In Revenues On The Back Of CRM Segment". *Forbes.Com.* https://www.forbes.com/sites/greatspeculations/2019/01/14/salesforce-com-to-post-13-billion-in-revenues-on-the-back-of-crm-segment/.

Wayland, Michael. 2019. "Cadillac's Revived Subscription Program To Rely On Dealers". *Automotive News.* https://www.autonews.com/dealers/cadillacs-revived-subscription-program-rely-dealers.

Whitler, Kimberly A. 2016. "How The Subscription Economy Is Disrupting The Traditional Business Model".

Forbes.Com. https://www.forbes.com/sites/kimberlywhit-ler/2016/01/17/a-new-business-trend-shifting-from-a-ser-vice-model-to-a-subscription-based-model/#398419344a5f.

Wolff-Mann, Ethan. 2016. "Here's How To Buy Dollar Shave Club Razors For Less Money On Amazon". *Money.* http://money.com/money/4414610/dollar-shave-club-razors-dorco-amazon/.

III. TRANSPARENCY

CHAPTER 10. DISAGGREGATING TRANSPARENCY

Allen, Courtland. 2018. "Building The Company You Actu-ally Want To Work At With Joel Gascoigne Of Buffer". *Indiehackers.Com.* https://www.indiehackers.com/pod-cast/058-joel-gascoigne-of-buffer.

Alton, Larry. 2017. "How Transparency Became A Top Priority For Businesses, And Why You Should Care". *Entrepreneur.* https://www.entrepreneur.com/article/295739.

"Amazon EC2 Pricing". 2019. *Amazon Web Services, Inc..* https://aws.amazon.com/ec2/pricing/.

Fraser, Kristopher. 2016. "Oliver Cabell Launches, Empha-sizes Transparency Of Production Process". *Fashionunited.*

Com. https://fashionunited.com/news/business/oliver-ca-bell-launches-emphasizes-transparency-of-production-process/2016062811879.

Gascoigne, Joel. 2019. "Transparent Pricing: What Your Money Goes Toward With Buffer". *Buffer Open Blog*. https://open.buffer.com/transparent-pricing-buffer/.

Gerzema, John. 2010. "Inc.: Understanding The Consumer Of The Future". *John Gerzema*. http://www.johngerzema.com/articles/inc.

Griswold, Alison. 2016. "Uber Has Quietly Started To End Surge Pricing As We Know It". *Quartz*. https://qz.com/676502/uber-has-quietly-started-to-end-surge-pricing-as-we-know-it/.

"Hospital Prices Are Now Public". 2019. *The Economist*. https://www.economist.com/united-states/2019/01/12/hospital-prices-are-now-public.

Kappel, Mike. 2019. "Transparency In Business: 5 Ways To Build Trust". *Forbes.Com*. https://www.forbes.com/sites/mikekappel/2019/04/03/transparency-in-business-5-ways-to-build-trust.

O'Toole, Mike. 2016. "At Everlane, Transparent Is The New Black". *Forbes.Com*. https://www.forbes.com/sites/mike-otoole/2016/01/05/at-everlane-transparent-is-the-new-black/.

Perez, Sarah. 2016. "Capital One Acquires Online Price Tracker Paribus". *Techcrunch*. https://techcrunch.com/2016/10/06/capital-one-acquires-online-price-tracker-paribus/.

Rosenthal, Elizabeth. 2014. "As Insurers Try To Limit Costs, Providers Hit Patients With More Separate Fees". *The New York Times*. https://www.nytimes.com/2014/10/26/us/as-insurers-try-to-limit-costs-providers-hit-patients-with-more-separate-fees.html.

Segran, Elizabeth. 2016. "Oliver Cabell Wants To Disrupt The Luxury Fashion Market". *Fast Company*. https://www.fast-company.com/3061376/oliver-cabell-wants-to-disrupt-the-luxury-fashion-market.

"The Benefits Of Cost Transparency". 2014. *Forbes.Com*. https://www.forbes.com/sites/hbsworkingknowledge/2014/12/15/when-retailers-reveal-production-costs-consumers-are-more-likely-to-buy/.

"Upfront Fares: No Math, No Surprises". 2016. *Uber Blog*. https://www.uber.com/blog/new-york-city/upfront-fares/.

Waber, Ben. 2018. "Radical Transparency Sounds Great Until You Consider The Research". *Quartz At Work*. https://qz.com/work/1195697/radical-transparency-sounds-great-until-you-consider-the-research/.

Westra, Kyle T. 2016a. "Does Surge Pricing Have An Image Problem?". *The Wiglaf Journal*. https://www.wiglafjournal.com/marketing/2016/01/does-surge-pricing-have-an-image-problem/.

Westra, Kyle T. 2016b. "Price Transparency Vs. Pricing Transparency". *The Wiglaf Journal*. https://www.wiglafjournal.com/pricing/2016/10/price-transparency-vs-pricing-transparency/.

"What Is AWS". 2019. *Amazon Web Services, Inc.*. https://aws.amazon.com/what-is-aws/.

CHAPTER 11. TRANSPARENCY AS A TOOL

Akerlof, George A. 1970. "The Market For "Lemons": Quality Uncertainty And The Market Mechanism". *The Quarterly Journal Of Economics* 84 (3): 488-500. https://www.jstor.org/stable/1879431.

Akerlof, George A., and Robert J. Shiller. 2015. *Phishing For Phools: The Economics Of Manipulation And Deception.* Princeton: Princeton University Press.

Jean, Sheryl. 2015. "Southwest Creates New Word 'Transfarency' For New Advertising Campaign". *Dallasnews.Com.* https://www.dallasnews.com/business/airlines/2015/10/08/southwest-creates-new-word-transfarency-for-new-advertising-campaign.

Martin, Matthew, Dinesh Nair, and Nour Al Ali. 2019. "Uber To Seal $3.1 Billion Deal To Buy Careem This Week". *Bloomberg.Com.* https://www.bloomberg.com/news/articles/2019-03-24/uber-is-said-to-seal-3-1-billion-deal-to-buy-careem-this-week.

McParland, Tom. 2017. "Here's The Problem With Those 'No Haggle' Dealerships". *Jalopnik.Com.* https://jalopnik.com/heres-the-problem-with-those-no-haggle-dealerships-1819136476.

Mohammed, Rafi. 2019. "It'S Time To Ban Hidden Fees". *Harvard Business Review.* https://hbr.org/2019/02/its-time-to-ban-hidden-fees.

Stein, Len. 2017. "The Key To Brand Design Is "Deliberate Differentiation"". *Brandingmag.* https://www.brandingmag.

com/2017/12/18/the-key-to-brand-design-is-deliberate-dif-
ferentiation/.

"Transfarency - Southwest Airlines". 2019. *Southwest.Com*.
https://www.southwest.com/html/air/transfarency/.

Westra, Kyle T. 2016. "Price Transparency Vs. Pricing Transparency". *The Wiglaf Journal*. https://www.wiglafjournal.
com/pricing/2016/10/price-transparency-vs-pricing-trans-
parency/.

CHAPTER 12. HIGHLIGHTING VALUE

Hirsch, Lauren. 2019. "Payless Shoesource Files For Bankruptcy As It Closes Its 2,500 US Stores". *CNBC*. https://
www.cnbc.com/2019/02/19/payless-shoesource-files-for-
bankruptcy-closes-its-2500-us-stores.html.

Kendall, Frank. 2018. "Boeing And The Navy Place A Big, Risky
Bet On The MQ-25 Unmanned Air Vehicle". *Forbes.Com*.
https://www.forbes.com/sites/frankkendall/2018/09/12/
boeing-and-the-navy-place-a-big-and-risky-bet-on-the-mq-
25-unmanned-air-vehicle/.

Lambert, Fred. 2018. "Tesla Reduces Price Of Model 3 Performance". *Electrek*. https://electrek.co/2018/10/26/tesla-mod-
el-3-performance-price-punish-reservation-holders/.

Lambert, Fred. 2019. "Tesla Owners Block Factory Entrance In Protest Over Model 3 Price Drop - Electrek". *Electrek.* https://electrek.co/2019/06/09/tesla-owners-protest-factory-model-3-price-drop/.

Lee, Timothy. 2019. "Tesla Slashes Prices For "Full Self-Driving," Won'T Refund Preorders". *Ars Technica.* https://arstechnica.com/cars/2019/03/price-cuts-anger-some-tesla-customers-who-preordered-full-self-driving/.

"Model 3 Performance "Upgrade Package" Is Now Free.". 2018. *Reddit.* https://www.reddit.com/r/teslamotors/comments/9rqaed/model_3_performance_upgrade_package_is_now_free/e8iua50/.

Nelson, Amanda. 2016. "15 Seth Godin Quotes To Fuel Spectacular Growth". *Salesforce Blog.* https://www.salesforce.com/blog/2016/06/seth-godin-quotes.html.

Obermiller, Carl, David Arnesen, and Marc Cohen. 2012. "Customized Pricing: Win-Win Or End Run?". *Drake Management Review* 1 (2). http://faculty.cbpa.drake.edu/dmr/0102/DMR010204R.pdf.

Phillips, Kristine. 2018. "'They Had Us Fooled': Inside Payless'S Elaborate Prank To Dupe People Into Paying $600 For Shoes". *The Washington Post.* https://www.washington-

post.com/business/2018/11/30/they-had-us-fooled-inside-
paylesss-elaborate-prank-dupe-people-into-paying-shoes/.

Salter, Chuck. 2009. "Kindle 2 Preview: Jeff Bezos On Why
Amazon Works Backwards". *Fast Company.* https://www.
fastcompany.com/90184288/kindle-2-preview-jeff-bezos-
on-why-amazon-works-backwards.

Walker, Tim. 2017. "How Much ...? The Rise Of Dynamic
And Personalised Pricing". *The Guardian.* https://www.
theguardian.com/global/2017/nov/20/dynamic-person-
alised-pricing.

IV. CHANNEL

CHAPTER 13. CHANNEL PARTNERS

Bech, Hans Peter. 2015. *Building Successful Partner Channels
In The Software Industry.* Klampenborg: TBK Publishing.

Coppola, Gabrielle. 2019. "Is Tesla A Cult? A Dealer Wonders
As Elon Musk Takes Bite Out Of BMW". *Fortune.* http://
fortune.com/2019/02/21/tesla-sales-bmw/.

Khemlani, Anjalee. 2019. "Bill Could Help Tesla Expand Number Of Dealerships In N.J. - ROI-NJ". *ROI-NJ.* http://www.

roi-nj.com/2019/02/14/industry/bill-could-help-tesla-expand-number-of-dealerships-in-n-j/.

Popper, Ben. 2014. "Auto Dealers Fire Back At Tesla CEO: 'This Musk Guy, He Wants All The Profits For Himself'". *The Verge.* https://www.theverge.com/2014/3/19/5525544/new-jersey-auto-dealers-respond-to-teslas-elon-musk.

Popper, Ben. 2015. "In Major Reversal, New Jersey Allows Tesla To Sell Its Cars Directly, Without Dealerships". *The Verge.* https://www.theverge.com/2015/3/18/8251821/tesla-new-jersey-direct-sales-dealerships-christie.

Welch, Chris. 2014. "Tesla Sales Will Be Banned In New Jersey Starting April 1st". *The Verge.* https://www.theverge.com/2014/3/11/5497638/tesla-sales-banned-in-new-jersey.

CHAPTER 14. CHANNEL AS A CHOICE

Chafkin, Max. 2007. "Entrepreneur Of The Year, 2007: Elon Musk". *Inc.Com.* https://www.inc.com/magazine/20071201/entrepreneur-of-the-year-elon-musk.html.

DeBord, Matthew. 2017. "Ford Is Undergoing A Huge Business Transformation—But Its Future Still Includes Dealers". *Business Insider.* https://www.businessinsider.com/ford-ceo-says-business-changing-dealer-network-2017-1.

Ellig, Jerry, and Jesse Martinez. 2015. "These Laws Should Hit The Road". *US News.* https://www.usnews.com/opinion/economic-intelligence/2015/01/19/laws-protecting-auto-franchises-are-bad-for-consumers-and-innovation.

Entis, Laura. 2018. "How To Create A Great Brand For Your Small Business". *Fortune.* http://fortune.com/2018/04/16/how-to-create-a-great-brand-for-your-small-business/.

Ferris, Robert. 2019. "Early Tesla Investor Defends Elon Musk As Tesla Shares Fall 10%: Musk Created 'The Iphone Of The Electric-Car Market'". *CNBC.* https://www.cnbc.com/2019/01/18/tesla-created-the-iphone-of-the-electric-car-market-says-investor.html.

"Find Us". 2018. *Tesla.Com.* https://www.tesla.com/findus.

"How Ordering Works". 2019. *Tesla.Com.* https://www.tesla.com/support/how-ordering-works.

Jeffs, Mike. 2015. "Customer Experience Study Identifies Expectation Gap Between Dealers And Consumers". *Drivingsales.* https://www.drivingsales.com/drivingsales/blog/20150331-drivingsales-customer-experience-study-identifies-expectation-gap-between-dealers-consumers.

Kaemingk, Diana. 2018. "How Tesla Drives Top Customer Experiences". *Qualtrics*. https://www.qualtrics.com/blog/tesla-customer-experience/.

Lambert, Fred. 2018. "Tesla Is Currently Fighting For The Right To Sell Its Cars Directly In 8 States". *Electrek*. https://electrek.co/2018/02/14/tesla-pushing-right-to-sell-cars-directly-states/.

Lunden, Ingrid. 2019. "Tesla U-Turns On Store Strategy, Will Keep Half Of Showrooms Open... And Hike Prices By 3%". *Techcrunch*. https://techcrunch.com/2019/03/11/tesla-showrooms/.

Matousek, Mark. 2019. "We Visited A Tesla Store And A Mercedes-Benz Dealership — These Are The Most Striking Differences Between Them". *Business Insider*. https://www.businessinsider.com/tesla-showroom-and-mercedes-dealership-comparison-pictures-2018-4.

McCorvey, J.J. 2016. "Road Rules: How Tesla Plans To Change The Way We Buy Cars". *Fast Company*. https://www.fastcompany.com/3062100/road-rules-how-tesla-plans-to-change-the-way-we-buy-cars.

Musk, Elon. 2014. "To The People Of New Jersey". *Tesla.Com*. https://www.tesla.com/blog/people-new-jersey.

O'Kane, Sean. 2019. "Tesla'S Promised $35,000 Model 3 Is Finally Here". *The Verge.* https://www.theverge.com/2019/2/28/18245165/tesla-model-3-price-lower-cost-elon-musk-news.

"Oatfinder". 2019. *Oatfinder.* https://oatfinder.oatly.com/.

Orlow, Emma. 2018. "How Oatly Became America's Trendiest Plant Milk". *Vice.* https://www.vice.com/en_us/article/pax8dz/how-oatly-became-americas-trendiest-plant-milk.

Popper, Ben. 2014. "Auto Dealers Fire Back At Tesla CEO: 'This Musk Guy, He Wants All The Profits For Himself'". *The Verge.* https://www.theverge.com/2014/3/19/5525544/new-jersey-auto-dealers-respond-to-teslas-elon-musk.

Settembre, Jeanette, and Alisa Wolfson. 2018. "People Are Hawking Oat Milk For More Than $200 On Amazon". *Marketwatch.* https://www.marketwatch.com/story/oat-milk-is-the-new-almond-milk-2018-09-27.

Sheetz, Michael. 2019. "Morgan Stanley Says Automakers Want To Sell Cars Like Tesla Does But Can't: 'It's Against The Law'". CNBC. https://www.cnbc.com/2019/03/05/morgan-stanley-against-the-law-for-automakers-to-sell-cars-like-tesla-does.html.

"Tesla Becomes First U.S. Auto IPO Since Ford". 2010. *Motor-trend*. https://www.motortrend.com/news/tesla-becomes-first-us-auto-ipo-since-ford/.

Thomson, Julie R. 2017. "You Wouldn't Believe How Hard It Is To Get Your Product Sold By Whole Foods". *Huffpost. Com*. https://www.huffpost.com/entry/how-to-get-into-whole-foods_n_59133a65e4b05e1ca203e910.

"Toni TV - Wow No Cow". 2017. *Youtube*. https://www.youtube.com/watch?v=_HQU0MB0D5A.

"US Tesla Service Centers". 2018. *Tesla.Com*. https://www.tesla.com/findus/list/services/United%20States.

Weissman, Cale Guthrie. 2019. "How Swedish Oat Milk Exploded Into A $15 Million Business Last Year". *Fast Company*. https://www.fastcompany.com/90298942/oatly-most-innovative-companies-2019.

Wertheim, Bonnie. 2018. "The Humble Ascent Of Oat Milk". *The New York Times*. https://www.nytimes.com/2018/01/19/style/oat-milk-coffee-oatly.html.

"Where Does The Car Dealer Make Money?". 2019. *Edmunds. Com*. https://www.edmunds.com/car-buying/where-does-the-car-dealer-make-money.html.

"Why Texas Bans The Sale Of Tesla Cars". 2013. *Yahoo! News.* https://news.yahoo.com/blogs/nightline-fix-abc-news/why-texas-bans-sale-tesla-cars-140842349.html.

CHAPTER 15. THE ELEPHANTS IN THE ROOM

"Amazon's Ambitious Drive Into Digital-Advertising". 2018. *The Economist.* https://www.economist.com/business/2018/10/27/amazons-ambitious-drive-into-digital-advertising.

Bennett, Bo. 2018. *Year To Success: When It Comes To Success, There Are No Shortcuts.* eBookIt.com.

Ek, Daniel. 2019. "Consumers And Innovators Win On A Level Playing Field". *Spotify Newsroom.* https://newsroom.spotify.com/2019-03-13/consumers-and-innovators-win-on-a-level-playing-field/.

Foster, Tom. 2017. "Warby Parker Grew To $250 Million In Sales Through Disciplined Growth. Now It's Time To Get Aggressive". *Inc.Com.* https://www.inc.com/magazine/201706/tom-foster/warby-parker-eyewear.html.

Hobica, George. 2017. "Why Airlines Shun Third-Party Travel Sites — And You Shouldn't". *Usatoday.Com.* https://www.

usatoday.com/story/travel/columnist/hobica/2017/10/31/
third-party-travel-sites/813866001/.

Isaac, Mike. 2014. "Where Profit Margins Are Hefty, Online
Upstarts Muscle In". *The New York Times*. https://www.
nytimes.com/2014/09/24/technology/24shave.html.

Jet, Johnny. 2017. "Is It Cheaper To Book Hotels Directly Or
Through Third Party Travel Sites?". *Forbes.Com*. https://
www.forbes.com/sites/johnnyjet/2017/08/28/is-it-cheap-
er-to-book-hotels-directly-or-through-third-party-travel-
sites/.

Kee Jr., Thomas H. 2018. "Amazon Is Losing Billions From
Its Retail Business And Rivals Should Be Scared". *Thestreet*. https://www.thestreet.com/opinion/amazon-is-los-
ing-money-from-retail-operations-14571703.

Komfo. 2018. "A Talk With Oatly". *Medium*. https://medium.
com/komfo-talks/a-talk-with-oatly-49080faa889c.

Ladd, Brittain. 2018. "Playing To Its Strengths: Why Walmart
Must Focus On Its Stores And Logistics". *Forbes.Com*.
https://www.forbes.com/sites/brittainladd/2018/09/09/
playing-to-its-strengths-why-walmart-must-focus-on-
groceries-stores-and-logistics/.

Lane, Sam. 2017. "How Tech Giants Have Shredded Our Privacy And What We Should Do About It". *PBS Newshour*. https://www.pbs.org/newshour/economy/tech-giants-shredded-privacy.

Martin, Grant. 2015. "Delta Air Lines Goes To War With Travel Agents". *Forbes.Com*. https://www.forbes.com/sites/grantmartin/2015/05/23/delta-air-lines-goes-to-war-with-travel-agents/.

McCorvey, J.J. 2016. "Road Rules: How Tesla Plans To Change The Way We Buy Cars". *Fast Company*. https://www.fastcompany.com/3062100/road-rules-how-tesla-plans-to-change-the-way-we-buy-cars.

Orlic, Matt. 2016. "6 Red Flags Warning Your Business Partner Will Drag You Down". *Entrepreneur*. https://www.entrepreneur.com/article/278532.

V. DATA

CHAPTER 16. THE NEW OIL

"Alibaba's Ma Says Data Resource Is Oil, Water Of The Future". 2015. *Bloomberg.Com*. https://www.bloomberg.com/news/articles/2015-10-14/alibaba-s-ma-says-data-resource-is-oil-water-of-the-future.

"Amazon Mechanical Turk". 2019. *Mturk.Com.* https://www.mturk.com/.

"Amazon's Empire Rests On Its Low-Key Approach To AI". 2019. *The Economist.* https://www.economist.com/business/2019/04/13/amazons-empire-rests-on-its-low-key-approach-to-ai.

"Billboards Are An Old But Booming Ad Medium". 2018. *The Economist.* https://www.economist.com/business/2018/11/08/billboards-are-an-old-but-booming-ad-medium.

Burns, Janet. 2019. "Uber And Lyft Won't Admit What They Are". *Forbes.Com.* https://www.forbes.com/sites/janetwburns/2019/03/20/uber-and-lyft-dont-know-what-they-are-courts-have-some-ideas/.

Chapman, Glenn. 2019. "With IPO Due, Uber Aims To Be 'Amazon Of Transportation'". *Phys.Org.* https://phys.org/news/2019-03-ipo-due-uber-aims-amazon.html.

"Dataage 2025 - The Digitization Of The World". 2019. *Seagate US.* https://www.seagate.com/our-story/data-age-2025/.

Dickey, Megan Rose. 2018. "Uber Acquires Bike-Share Startup JUMP". *Techcrunch*. https://techcrunch.com/2018/04/09/uber-acquires-bike-share-startup-jump/.

Foroohar, Rana. 2019. "Big Tech Must Pay For Access To America'S 'Digital Oil'". *FT.Com*. https://www.ft.com/content/fd3d885c-579d-11e9-a3db-1fe89bedc16e.

Goldstein, Jacob. 2014. "To Increase Productivity, UPS Monitors Drivers' Every Move". *Planet Money : NPR*. https://www.npr.org/sections/money/2014/04/17/303770907/to-increase-productivity-ups-monitors-drivers-every-move.

"How Regulators Can Prevent Excessive Concentration Online". 2018. *The Economist*. https://www.economist.com/special-report/2018/06/28/how-regulators-can-prevent-excessive-concentration-online.

Kline, Daniel B. 2017. "Jeff Bezos Says It Will Always Be "Day 1" At Amazon". *The Motley Fool*. https://www.fool.com/investing/2017/04/13/jeff-bezos-says-it-will-always-be-day-1-at-amazon.aspx.

Morgan, Jacob. 2014. "A Simple Explanation Of 'The Internet Of Things'". *Forbes.Com*. https://www.forbes.com/sites/jacobmorgan/2014/05/13/simple-explanation-internet-things-that-anyone-can-understand/.

Munger, Michael C. 2018. *Tomorrow 3.0: Transaction Costs And The Sharing Economy*. New York: Cambridge University Press.

Rapolu, Bhoopathi. 2016. "Internet Of Aircraft Things: An Industry Set To Be Transformed". *Aviation Week*. https://aviationweek.com/connected-aerospace/internet-aircraft-things-industry-set-be-transformed.

Ryan, Kevin J. 2018. "The Tech That Powers Your Self-Driving Car Might Be Built Using People Playing Games On Their Phones". *Inc.Com*. https://www.inc.com/kevin-j-ryan/self-driving-cars-powered-by-people-playing-games-mighty-ai.html.

Schmarzo, Bill. 2019. "Data Curation: Weaving Raw Data Into Business Gold". *Linkedin Pulse*. https://www.linkedin.com/pulse/data-curation-weaving-raw-business-gold-bill-schmarzo/.

Soper, Taylor. 2017. "Spare5 Re-Launches As Mighty AI, Raises $14M From Intel, Accenture, Google For AI Training Data Service". *Geekwire*. https://www.geekwire.com/2017/spare5-re-launches-mighty-ai-raises-14m-intel-accenture-google-ai-training-data-service/.

Stewart, Jack. 2017. "The Human Army Using Phones To Teach AI To Drive". *WIRED*. https://www.wired.com/story/mighty-ai-training-self-driving-cars/.

Stoll, John D. 2019. "Why Investors Don'T Care That Snap And Lyft Are Hemorrhaging Money". *WSJ*. https://www.wsj.com/articles/why-investors-dont-care-that-snap-and-lyft-are-hemorrhaging-money-11556289952.

Webb, Alex. 2019. "What Does Uber Love More: Restaurants Or Investors?". *Bloomberg.Com*. https://www.bloomberg.com/opinion/articles/2019-04-21/what-does-uber-eats-love-more-restaurants-or-investors.

CHAPTER 17. MONETIZING DATA SERVICES

"Amazon's Empire Rests On Its Low-Key Approach To AI". 2019. *The Economist*. https://www.economist.com/business/2019/04/13/amazons-empire-rests-on-its-low-key-approach-to-ai.

Burgess, Matt. 2018. "This Is How Netflix's Secret Recommendation System Works". *WIRED UK*. https://www.wired.co.uk/article/netflix-data-personalisation-watching.

"Data Is Giving Rise To A New Economy". 2017. *The Economist.*
https://www.economist.com/briefing/2017/05/06/data-is-
giving-rise-to-a-new-economy.

Fowler, Geoffrey A. 2019. "It'S The Middle Of The Night.
Do You Know Who Your Iphone Is Talking To?". *The
Washington Post.* https://www.washingtonpost.com/tech-
nology/2019/05/28/its-middle-night-do-you-know-who-
your-iphone-is-talking/.

Garcia Martinez, Antonio. 2019. "I'm An Ex-Facebook Exec:
Don't Believe What They Tell You About Ads". *The
Guardian.* https://www.theguardian.com/technology/2017/
may/02/facebook-executive-advertising-data-comment.

Grady, Denise. 2019. "A.I. Took A Test To Detect Lung Cancer. It Got An A.". *The New York Times.* https://www.
nytimes.com/2019/05/20/health/cancer-artificial-intelli-
gence-ct-scans.html.

Kelly, Heather. 2018. "Google's Data Collection Is Hard To
Escape, Study Claims". *Cnnmoney.* https://money.cnn.
com/2018/08/21/technology/google-data-collection/index.
html.

Kushal, Avanish, Sharmadha Moorthy, and Vikash Kumar.
2011. "Pricing For Data Markets". https://pdfs.semantic-

scholar.org/93c7/0f67a329279afe66a753252f546642a0e1aa.
pdf.

LaForgia, Michael, Matthew Rosenberg, and Gabriel J.X.
Dance. 2019. "Facebook'S Data Deals Are Under Criminal
Investigation". *The New York Times.* https://www.nytimes.
com/2019/03/13/technology/facebook-data-deals-investiga-
tion.html.

Levitt, Theodore. 1969. *The Marketing Mode: Pathways To Corporate Growth By Theodore Levitt.* McGraw-Hill.

"New Ways To Trade Data". 2018. *The Economist.* https://www.
economist.com/science-and-technology/2018/03/28/new-
ways-to-trade-data.

Pressman, Aaron, and Adam Lashinsky. 2018. "Ata Sheet—
Why Netflix Isn't Really A Tech Company". *Fortune.*
http://fortune.com/2018/04/17/data-sheet-netflix-priva-
cy-data-facebook/.

Schuman, Evan. 2017. "Digital Transformation: How Machine
Learning Could Help Change Business". *Ars Technica.*
https://arstechnica.com/information-technology/2017/09/
digital-transformation-1/.

CHAPTER 18. KNOWING THE CUSTOMER

Abbey, James, Michael Ketzenberg, and Richard Metters. 2018.
"A More Profitable Approach To Product Returns". *MIT
Sloan Management Review*. https://sloanreview.mit.edu/
article/a-more-profitable-approach-to-product-returns/.

Gorman, Shawn O. 2018. "A Letter To Our Customers -
L.L.Bean". *Facebook.Com*. https://www.facebook.com/
llbean/posts/a-letter-to-our-customerssince-1912-our-mis-
sion-has-been-to-sell-high-quality-pr/10155636619902415/.

Govindarajan, Vijay, and Jeffrey R. Immelt. 2019. "The Only
Way Manufacturers Can Survive". *MIT Sloan Management Review*. https://sloanreview.mit.edu/article/the-on-
ly-way-manufacturers-can-survive.

"L.L. Bean - Easy Returns And Exchanges". 2019. *L.L. Bean*.
https://www.llbean.com/llb/shop/510624.

Lam, Bourree. 2015. "Why L.L. Bean's Boots Keep Selling Out". *The Atlantic*. https://www.theatlantic.com/
business/archive/2015/10/llbean-duck-boot-labor-shoes-
maine/410863/.

Levitt, Theodore. 2008. *Marketing Myopia*. Boston: Harvard
Business Press.

Nash, Kim S. 2018a. "L.L. Bean To Link Boots, Coats To A Blockchain". *WSJ*. https://blogs.wsj.com/cio/2018/02/07/l-l-bean-to-link-boots-coats-to-a-blockchain/.

Nash, Kim S. 2018b. "L.L. Bean Cancels Internet Of Things Project". *WSJ*. https://blogs.wsj.com/cio/2018/03/14/l-l-bean-cancels-internet-of-things-project/.

Ross, Jeanne W., Cynthia M. Beath, and Anne Quaadgras. 2013. "You May Not Need Big Data After All". *Harvard Business Review*. https://hbr.org/2013/12/you-may-not-need-big-data-after-all.

Sherman, Erik. 2018. "L.L. Bean Will Use Blockchain Tech To See How Often You Wash Your Clothes". *Inc.Com*. https://www.inc.com/erik-sherman/ll-beans-new-iot-blockchain-tech-combo-is-very-smart-and-incredibly-creepy.html.

Smiley, Lauren. 2019. "Stitch Fix'S Radical Data-Driven Way To Sell Clothes–$1.2 Billion Last Year–Is Reinventing Retail". *Fast Company*. https://www.fastcompany.com/90298900/stitch-fix-most-innovative-companies-2019.

Stevens, Khadeeja. 2018. "Banned From Amazon: The Shoppers Who Make Too Many Returns". *WSJ*. https://www.wsj.com/articles/banned-from-amazon-the-shoppers-who-make-too-many-returns-1526981401.

"The Growth Of Microbrands Threatens Consumer-Goods Giants". 2018. *The Economist*. https://www.economist.com/business/2018/11/08/the-growth-of-microbrands-threatens-consumer-goods-giants.

"The Making Of An American Icon". 2019. *L.L. Bean*. https://www.llbean.com/llb/shop/506697.

CONCLUSION

CHAPTER 19. TYING IT TOGETHER

Bezos, Jeffrey P. 2017. "2016 Letter To Shareholders". *Amazon Day One Blog*. https://blog.aboutamazon.com/company-news/2016-letter-to-shareholders.

Holiday, Ryan. 2014. *The Obstacle Is The Way: The Timeless Art Of Turning Trials Into Triumph*. 1st ed. New York: Portfolio.

CHAPTER 20. FOCUS ON CUSTOMERS

Adair, Paul. 2019. "Focusing On The Customer Experience Drives Sales And Margin Performance". Presentation, Professional Pricing Society Spring Conference, Atlanta, GA, 2019.

Bariso, Justin. 2017. "A Tesla Customer Complained On Twitter. Less Than 30 Minutes Later, Elon Musk Promised To Fix It". *Inc.Com*. https://www.inc.com/justin-bariso/elon-musk-promises-to-implement-customer-suggestio.html.

Bezos, Jeffrey P. 2017. "2016 Letter To Shareholders". *Amazon Day One Blog*. https://blog.aboutamazon.com/company-news/2016-letter-to-shareholders.

Garbuio, Massimo, and Nidthida Lin. 2018. "Artificial Intelligence As A Growth Engine For Health Care Startups: Emerging Business Models". *California Management Review* 61 (2). https://journals.sagepub.com/doi/10.1177/0008125618811931.

Hyken, Shep. 2019. "Customer Service And CX Lessons From Three Iconic Brands". *Hyken.Com*. https://hyken.com/blog-app/customer-service-cx-lessons-iconic-brands/.

MacMillan, Jeffrey. 2019. "Aligning Pricing With Customer Value: Transitioning To Usage-Based Models". Presentation, Professional Pricing Society Spring Conference, Atlanta, GA, 2019.

Martin, Roger L. 2019. "Pricing Needs To Reflect Who People Want To Be, Not Just What They Want". *Harvard*

Business Review. https://hbr.org/2019/01/pricing-needs-to-reflect-who-people-want-to-be-not-just-what-they-want.

Poyar, Kyle. 2019. "It's A Rough Time To Be A Startup - Here's What You Can Do About It". *OpenView.* https://openview-partners.com/blog/its-a-rough-time-to-be-a-startup-heres-what-you-can-do-about-it/.

Treacy, Michael, and Fred Wiersema. 1993. "Customer Intimacy And Other Value Disciplines". *Harvard Business Review.* https://hbr.org/1993/01/customer-intimacy-and-other-value-disciplines.

Yee, Stephanie. 2018. "Bridging The Gap Between Sales And Pricing". Presentation, Professional Pricing Society Fall Conference, Dallas, TX, 2018.

CHAPTER 21. FOCUS ON PROFITS

Brown, Eliot. 2019. "Uber, Lyft Ipos Might Lead To Higher Fares". *WSJ.* https://www.wsj.com/articles/why-the-uber-lyft-ipos-may-lead-to-higher-fares-11555925401.

Cuban, Mark. 2011. "The Most Patriotic Thing You Can Do". *Blogmaverick.Com.* http://blogmaverick.com/2011/09/19/the-most-patriotic-thing-you-can-do-2/.

Dickey, Megan Rose. 2019. "Ahead Of IPO, Airbnb Achieves Profitability For Second Year In A Row". *Techcrunch.* https://techcrunch.com/2019/01/15/ahead-of-ipo-airbnb-achieves-profitability-for-second-year-in-a-row/.

Drucker, Peter F. 1963. "Managing For Business Effectiveness". *Harvard Business Review.* https://hbr.org/1963/05/managing-for-business-effectiveness.

Ferris, Robert. 2019. "Elon Musk Was Optimistic Tesla Would Have A Profitable First Quarter. Now He Isn't. What Changed?". *CNBC.* https://www.cnbc.com/2019/03/01/elon-musk-thought-tesla-would-be-profitable-and-now-he-doesnt.html.

Ferriss, Tim. 2018. "The Tim Ferriss Show Transcripts: Doug Mcmillon (#345)". *The Blog Of Author Tim Ferriss.* https://tim.blog/2018/11/12/the-tim-ferriss-show-podcasts-doug-mcmillon/.

Ferriss, Tim. 2019. "The Tim Ferriss Show Transcripts: Eric Schmidt (#367)". *The Blog Of Author Tim Ferriss.* https://tim.blog/2019/04/11/the-tim-ferriss-show-transcripts-eric-schmidt-367/.

Huang, Eustance. 2019. "Analysts Say Investors Should Avoid Shares Of China's Meituan Dianping". *CNBC.* https://

www.cnbc.com/2019/03/21/analysts-are-advising-investors-to-stay-away-from-meituan-dianping.html.

Manning, Jon. 2012. "Welcome To The Warren Buffett School Of Pricing". *Smartcompany*. https://www.smartcompany.com.au/people-human-resources/leadership/welcome-to-the-warren-buffett-school-of-pricing/.

"Matt Levine Live At Bloomberg HQ (Ep. 34)". 2019. *Medium*. https://medium.com/conversations-with-tyler/matt-levine-tyler-cowen-finance-bitcoin-19e380b7430.

"Riding Alone In A Car Is A Luxury—An Increasingly Unaffordable One". 2019. *The Economist*. https://www.economist.com/finance-and-economics/2019/05/09/riding-alone-in-a-car-is-a-luxury-an-increasingly-unaffordable-one.

Sozzi, Brian. 2019. "Walmart CEO: Autonomous-Car Delivery Is Part Of Our Future". *Yahoo! Finance*. https://finance.yahoo.com/news/walmart-ceo-autonomouscar-delivery-is-part-of-our-future-125143113.html.

Stone, Brad. 2017. *The Upstarts: How Uber, Airbnb, And The Killer Companies Of The New Silicon Valley Are Changing The World*. Little, Brown and Company.

CHAPTER 22. PARTING THOUGHTS

Haden, Jeff. 2017. "20 Years Ago, Jeff Bezos Said This 1 Thing Separates People Who Achieve Lasting Success From Those Who Don't". *Inc.Com*. https://www.inc.com/jeff-haden/20-years-ago-jeff-bezos-said-this-1-thing-separates-people-who-achieve-lasting-success-from-those-who-dont.html.

Williamson, John N. 1986. *The Leader Manager*. New York: Wiley.

INDEX

A

machine 71, 74, 78, 134, 141, 151,
250, 256, 258, 259, 269, 281
machine learning 74, 256,
259, 269
MacLennan, David 73
MacMillan, Jeff 294
Macquarie University 296
Macy's 118
Maine 275
Main Street Genome 63, 91, 251
maintenance 21, 152, 232, 253, 281
Malik, Om 29
management 49, 50, 55, 64, 110,
136, 139, 142, 149, 169, 179, 206,
215, 243, 247, 250, 278, 280,
282, 290, 292, 307
manager 75, 77, 151, 240, 252
manipulate 79, 201
manufacturers 40, 52, 94, 146, 147,
152, 156, 204, 220, 221, 240, 281
manufacturing 146, 243, 275
margin 15, 118, 133, 148, 171, 179,
188, 196, 198, 216, 228, 231, 233,
305, 309, 312
marginal cost 100, 197, 198, 206
margins 133, 140, 146, 206, 237,
254, 308
market capitalization 13, 65, 305
market dynamics 39, 93
Market for "Lemons" 189, 190
marketing 33, 51, 124, 163, 187, 193,
198, 199, 201, 202, 206, 213, 217,
222, 270, 271, 294, 298, 310, 311
market-making 188
markets 14, 15, 21, 22, 28, 32, 35,
42, 46, 56–58, 61, 62, 65, 67,

70–72, 77, 78, 80, 84, 93, 115,
117, 119, 168, 184, 188–191, 193,
236, 281, 287, 293, 297, 298, 313
Marriott 31
Martin, Roger L. 291
Mason, Andrew 44
Mathur, Raghav 153
maximization (see: profit maximization)
MBA 15, 40, 44
McLean, Matt 151
McMillon, Doug 306
measurements 127, 154, 191, 249
Mechanical Turk 255, 256
media 29, 37, 39, 41, 42, 169, 240,
271, 272, 276, 295
medical 97, 172, 197, 269, 296
Medicare 46
Meituan-Dianping 305
membership 11, 157, 299
menu 94, 200, 202
menu costs 94
merchandise 77, 241
merchants 43, 66, 105, 108, 109,
119, 122–124, 130
metered pricing 7, 145, 154–159,
167–169, 240, 263
methodologies 154, 175, 199, 201
metrics 157, 262–264
Mexico 117
microbrand 279
Microsoft 27, 31, 38, 39, 65, 149,
248, 249, 296
Middleman Economy 32
middlemen 20, 28–30, 32, 34, 61,
67, 70, 78–80, 220

willingness to accept 117, 182
willingness to pay 98–100, 102,
    104, 106, 107, 109, 112, 116, 117,
    120, 121, 127–129, 189, 198, 199
Windows 27, 108, 110
workforce 72, 92, 112, 256
worse 104, 106, 165, 166, 177, 288
writing 14, 27, 29, 61, 62, 82, 92,
    119, 126, 158, 163, 173, 205, 220,

227, 235, 242, 247, 248, 251, 279,
    307, 310
wrong 12, 27, 28, 114, 157, 277, 294

Y

Yee, Stephanie 299
Yelp 33
Yungang Grottoes 117

CPSIA information can be obtained
at www.ICGtesting.com
Printed in the USA
LVHW040109290819
629362LV00007B/242/P